CAS
IS
KIN

CASH
IS
KING

MAINTAIN LIQUIDITY,

BUILD CAPITAL,

**AND PREPARE YOUR BUSINESS
FOR EVERY OPPORTUNITY**

PETER W. KINGMA

WILEY

Published by John Wiley & Sons, Inc., Hoboken, New Jersey.
Published simultaneously in Canada.

For general information on our other products and services or for technical support, please contact
our Customer Care Department within the United States at (800) 762-2974, outside the United States
at (317) 572-3993 or fax (317) 572-4002.

Wiley also publishes its books in a variety of electronic formats. Some content that appears in print
may not be available in electronic formats. For more information about Wiley products, visit our web
site at www.wiley.com.

Library of Congress Cataloging-in-Publication Data:

Names: Kingma, Peter W., author.
Title: Cash is king : maintain liquidity, build capital, and prepare your
   business for every opportunity / Peter W. Kingma.
Description: Hoboken, New Jersey : Wiley, [2024] | Includes index.
Identifiers: LCCN 2024001116 (print) | LCCN 2024001117 (ebook) | ISBN
   9781119983354 (cloth) | ISBN 9781119983378 (adobe pdf) | ISBN
   9781119983361 (epub)
Subjects: LCSH: Liquidity (Economics) | Cash management.
Classification: LCC HG178 .K56 2024 (print) | LCC HG178 (ebook) | DDC
   658.15/5—dc23/eng/20240214
LC record available at https://lccn.loc.gov/2024001116
LC ebook record available at https://lccn.loc.gov/2024001117

COVER DESIGN: PAUL MCCARTHY

SKY10069861_031724

Dedicated to the memory of my parents, Gordon and Barbara Kingma, and to my partner in life, Thom Lambert.

Contents

Contents

Introduction

Smartly dressed in a blue suit, white shirt, and a pocket square, matching his brilliant red tie, Lee Iacocca strode confidently into a House committee room to formally ask Congress for a bailout of the Chrysler Corporation. It was September 1979, and Iacocca, the newly installed chairman of Chrysler, was nearly as famous as the company he had started leading.

Chrysler was the 10th largest company in the United States, but the third of the big three automakers. It had a storied past filled with great innovations in engineering and design such as antilock brakes, key-start ignition, cruise control, and, perhaps most important, cup holders. But the 1960s and 1970s were hard on Chrysler. Attempts to expand globally coupled with several product failures left Chrysler very vulnerable going into the 1980s. The company did not have a balance sheet strong enough to weather three recessions, two oil crises, new environmental regulations, and soaring inflation. Chrysler simply did not have enough cash.

The seemingly simple concept of managing positive cash flow, on the *balance sheet*, trips up so many businesses. You must have enough cash on hand to pay your bills, invest in research, develop new products, build efficient plants and so on. Those with strong balance sheets are resilient and can take advantage of growth opportunities. Those who are too *leveraged*—too much debt and too little cash—are vulnerable any time the economy shifts. Despite its illustrious history, Chrysler could not keep up and needed a lifeline from the government.

There are many factors that go into making a business successful. Having products people want to buy, beating competition on price, and employing a talented and efficient labor force are critical. And there are often factors out of management's control. Inflation, increasing interest rates, supply chain disruptions, and geopolitical crises can make or break many businesses. As I write this book in 2023, the global economy has suffered one shock after another beyond any one company's control.

The COVID-19 pandemic has altered permanently how businesses operate. It laid bare the simple fact that the global supply chain is highly entangled. In 2020, consumer preferences shifted overnight, and even strong, resilient companies scrambled to keep up. This story continues to play out, and I'd argue that the norm for the next five-plus years is one of rapidly shifting supply-and-demand dynamics. Even things like our collective approach to global warming will create a high degree of volatility.

There are many things businesses must do to meet these challenges, but one factor is, without question, absolutely critical. Companies must have access to cash to address volatility.

I coauthored a study at Ernst & Young in 2022 that demonstrates a strong correlation between effective cash management and resiliency. We reviewed 5,000 global companies and evaluated how well they manage working capital. The upper half of those companies are 20+% more effective at limiting the initial shocks of market downturns. Further, weaker performing peers in the bottom half spend on average 26% more time after economic downturns lagging peers in terms of shareholder return. It takes cash to address market shocks.

When global supply chains collapsed at the onset of the pandemic, companies scrambled to adjust, investing heavily to secure materials and paying far more for logistics. Some used debt to fund their capital requirements. This worked as long as interest rates were low and the cost of debt was cheap. But, as the economy heated up and inflationary concerns were addressed through rising interest rates, the debt strategy became unsustainable. Organizations that entered this period with effective cash management discipline not only were better able to respond to market shocks but also they used their strong balance sheets to win market share from weaker rivals.

The market is never constant. There are always ups and downs. Smart leaders recognize this and are focused on cash management at all times. I describe this as having a *cash culture*. A company with a cash culture understands it is not just about revenue growth but also about cash generation. This is not as easy as it sounds.

Most businesses are built on a profit-and-loss (P&L) culture where sales rule. But things can get out of control very fast. For example, salespeople can agree to all sorts of terms and conditions. You won a big deal but can't get paid for 120 days. Purchasing can chase the lowest cost for material but in doing so agree to large quantities with long lead times. Manufacturing can operate plants most efficiently through long run cycles—running equipment at capacity—but your investment in inventory balloons. There are many examples of trade-offs management needs to make to keep equilibrium between the P&L and the balance sheet. Unfortunately, many of the decision rights for those trade-offs are scattered about the organization and are being made by individuals without insight into downstream effects.

Companies that truly have a cash culture ensure that people have the right tools and training to make good decisions. They promote processes and policies that improve cash generation.

And they align incentives and metrics to ensure compliance and sustainability.

Trade working capital accounts for the biggest component of operational cash flow. What is *trade working capital*? Simply put, it's current assets and current liabilities that are directly associated with operations. Current assets include inventory and accounts receivable, and current liabilities include accounts payable. A business buys materials, investing in inventory and creating products. The products are then sold to customers, and the amounts customers owe are referred to as *accounts receivable*. Conversely, the company will need to pay suppliers for the materials they buy, which is called *accounts payable*. Timing is at the heart of effective working capital management.

I'd like to align what I owe my suppliers with how I get paid from my customers and hope to hold only the inventory that I can quickly sell. The more inventory I start to hold, the more cash I tie up in my business. The longer it takes my customers to pay me, again, the more cash I tie up. And, if I must pay my vendors quickly for the materials I buy, I am making big cash outlays often in advance of when my customers will pay me. Let's say that my customers take four months to pay me and that it will take me six months to sell off all the inventory I bought, but the guys I owe money to are knocking on the door and they want to get paid . . . now. Depending on who these guys are, I might be in a real jam. The timing of when I must pay for stuff and when I get paid for my products or services is what makes or breaks my cash flow.

Okay. It's super-easy. Pay people slower, don't hold on to more inventory than I need, and get people to pay me faster. End of story—no need for this book!

Perhaps I'm a self-interested author, but it's not that easy. Businesses are complex entities. Markets are constantly changing. Decisions that make sense one day might be disturbing the next day. And, as I said, there is often a bias to chasing sales growth without much attention to that pesky art of timing.

This book is not a textbook.

Rest assured, there will be no fancy graphs or complicated equations. Instead, we'll look at what really drives cash through the lens of a fictious company, Owens Electrical. We'll meet the president, Bob, as well as run-of-the-mill employees who deal with everyday, real-life decisions. Sometimes they make good decisions, other times not so good. Through this story I hope that you come away with an appreciation for the importance of effectively managing working capital and operating cash flow.

In Chapter 1, we will look at how Owens is managing the money people owe them. This will be referred to as *order-to-cash* (OTC). These are the steps taken from the time an order is received through to getting the cash in hand. It includes activities such as order entry, billing, and collections. But, because things rarely go as planned, our team at Owens will need to straighten out mistakes they make that cause their customers to hold back payments.

Next, in Chapter 2, we will focus on how Owens is buying things from others. This is called *procure-to-pay* (PTP). It turns out there will be a lot of room for improvement from our team at Owens on this front. Then we start to look at where the big bucks are: inventory.

Inventory management is complicated and trips up even the best companies. You can earn bachelor's degrees, master's degrees, and PhDs studying this topic. Chapters 3 through 6 examine some drivers and best practices. Fear not, we'll keep it at a high-enough level to explore the concepts without (I hope) putting you to sleep.

Once we've covered the basics of working capital management, we will then consider what we should measure. I'll say it here and then again in Chapter 7: "What's measured improves."

Another, far more famous Peter wrote that—Mr. Peter Drucker. I agree completely. But metrics can be tricky. If we measure too few things, we might not get the outcomes we desire. But, if we overload the organization with too many metrics, we might confuse everyone and get similarly dismal outcomes. The key is to pick the right things to measure and to assign them to people who have direct impact. That's what we will look at in that chapter.

I said previously that I have empirical evidence that cash really is king and that companies with healthy cash flow are more resilient than their peers that don't have as strong a balance sheet. In Chapter 8, our friends at Owens will illustrate this point. Bob, the president of Owens, will then conclude that the business needs to truly transform and address all the issues covered in the first eight chapters. In Chapter 9, he will establish a cash leadership office. This will be the foundation to building and sustaining a true cash culture.

Last, before I let you go, in Chapter 10, we will look at how all of this applies to nonmanufacturing companies. Owens (our fictitious company) is a traditional manufacturer that mostly sells business-to-business. Although certainly not exhaustive, we'll consider other types of organizations and how these management principles apply.

So, who is this book for?

My hope is that anyone who is interested in management will find this book an interesting read. There is much written about sales, marketing, leadership, and even efficient operations. Aside from textbooks, there are few books that explain working capital and cash. So, this book is for middle managers who aspire to senior leadership, executives and directors who want to help their organizations understand the importance of cash, and investors who would like to better understand what makes a company truly healthy.

Frankly, it's for anyone interested in business.

CHAPTER

1

Order-to-Cash

Meet Bob. Bob runs a mid-size company, Owens Inc., that makes and sells electrical equipment. Bob joined Owens out of grad school and worked his way up from junior engineer to CEO. The company grew and evolved and in the past five years it has really taken off.

When he started, Bob knew just about everyone at Owens and prided himself on understanding most aspects of the business. But as president, he recognizes that Owens has become very complex, and he no longer has the same grasp on things he once had. Recently, a young man, Juan, introduced himself to Bob while in line in the company canteen. Bob saw his younger self in Juan and was impressed, thinking it was smart of Juan to strike up a conversation with the company president.

"What department are you in?" Juan then asked, bursting Bob's bubble. He had no idea who Bob was.

"So that is now how it is," Bob thought to himself. "This place has become so big that the president goes unrecognized in his own offices."

Growth at Owens, like most companies, has not always been smooth sailing. There was a time when the company almost lost its most important customer over quality problems. Then there was a sort of "bet the business" that Bob boldly made when he first became president. Bob plunged the company into new products and new markets, not knowing if the once sleepy business could keep up. These were trying periods for certain, but for the most part the company grew and grew. And as it did, leaders like Bob started to get complacent. The memories of what it took to keep a small business afloat, like the times of uncertainty about being able to make payroll in each month, had faded. The excitement of growth took hold.

There were ribbon-cutting ceremonies all over the country. Local officials courted Bob and praised his leadership. Investors loved the results, and it became quite intoxicating. Bob would hold operations reviews and started each meeting with graphs showing sales projections, challenging his team to keep the focus on growth. "The customer always comes first at Owens!" Bob would frequently extort. But what he meant by that was "sales to customers always comes first." There is a big difference.

Quarter after quarter, sales were growing, and Owens was taking market share. The future looked very bright, and Bob felt unstoppable. That is until Carol, the chief financial officer (CFO) of Owens, started to raise concerns about cash flow. She was concerned because interest rates were increasing, the complexity of their business was growing and the demand for capital improvements was at an all-time high. Inventory was growing faster than sales and although Bob did acknowledge some concern about that during operations meetings, it wasn't enough to tap on the brakes of growth. There was another big problem that had Carol very concerned. This one was really affecting her ability to forecast cash and to fund all the expensive capital initiatives Bob had launched. Customers were paying much slower than they had in the past.

Over the last three years their DSO (days sales outstanding) had increased from about 45 days to more than 65 days. That means it now takes Owens 20 more days—on average—to collect money from its customers. When Carol first started to tell Bob of the steady growth in DSO, he didn't seem all that alarmed. "We will get the money eventually—right? It's just a part of growing the business, Carol," Bob said rather dismissively.

Carol saw it quite differently. It was a warning siren. There was a time when her boss would have understood this. Years ago, Bob lost the chance to make a strategic investment because Owens's balance sheet was not healthy enough. He fumed and promised to not forget that valuable lesson. "Cash is king, Carol!" He would say, as if he needed to remind her. But managing cash is not always glamorous. It's not like sales. Sales are exciting. Winning a big contract, entering new markets—that's what gets called out and celebrated. Collecting a bill on time is boring. Like most business leaders, Bob delegated those tasks and focused his energy and attention on revenue.

They worked together for years and were quite close, but there was no mistaking who the boss was at Owens. And as the company—and by proxy Bob—became more successful, his leadership team often told Bob what he wanted to hear. Even the board of directors at Owens seldom challenged Bob. So, getting her boss to focus on the seemingly mundane topic of cash was going to take a deft approach. Carol would need to ease into it. Bob was an engineer by training so she would get him stimulated by the thought of solving complex problems. Just going up to Bob and asking him to talk about accounts receivable would be a non-starter. He was consumed lately with new product launches and expanding into Asia.

"You fix it!" She anticipated Bob would tell her. "Cash is a finance problem, and you are the CFO," he would remind her. But Carol knew differently. She knew that at the rate Owens was growing and with inventory piling up and customer collections taking much longer, this required executive leadership focus. "Cash really is king," she would need to remind her boss, but she'd certainly need to do that in a tactful, diplomatic way.

"Bob, we've become a bank," Carol blurted out during their weekly meeting. "And not a very good bank at that." So much for the tactful, ease-into it approach. Carol pulled out the pin and tossed the grenade.

"What are you talking about Carol? A bank?" Bob shrugged.

"Most of our customers have payment terms between 30 and 40 days. They are obligated to pay within that range after they receive the equipment. But, on average, they now pay us about 65 days after delivery. That means we are allowing them to hold onto our money an additional 25 to 35 days. We are sort of floating them loans. Oh, and the best part? There is no interest charge. We don't charge them anything additional for this float. We have become a not-for-profit bank, Bob."

A frown came across his face. "Well, why don't you get on the phone and call these guys and get this straightened out," Bob said sternly. Carol then explained that she had been in touch with many of the customers she personally knew, and they painted a different picture. A few sheepishly admitted that they were having cash issues and were delaying payments, but most explained that Owens either accepted new commercial terms or caused the delay because of billing problems. The 20 days increase in DSO—the time it takes to collect money—was self-inflicted.

"Bob, this is not a finance problem. It's an operations problem. We want to keep growing, but it takes capital to fund that growth. I don't know how to delicately says this, Bob, but we've taken our eye off the ball." This got a rise out of Bob. He prided himself on knowing the details of his business. Now his CFO was telling him that he was not focused on the right things? But to his credit, he allowed a decent pause before he responded.

"We go back a long way, Carol. I remember the nights we'd order pizzas and each of us would work the phones trying to chase down past due bills. It was sort of fun—those days. We had a vision. We were going to build something special. And we did. And over the years we've hired a small army of folks to manage billing and collections. We hardly took our eyes off the ball, Carol."

She knew that despite his calm tone, Bob was irritated. She was calling him out and it had been quite some time since anyone had done that so openly. "We could hire twice as many of those people, Bob, and I don't think we would achieve better results," she said carefully. "Look, what I'm trying to call attention to is that we have process breakdowns as a result of our rapid growth. Just like we've had to reconfigure our plants to accommodate growth, we need to update our business processes. This is what you do best, Bob. We need the engineer in you to help eliminate defects." Now she was luring him in. She knew that Bob loved to solve complex problems.

Carol walked over to the whiteboard and wrote the following:

- Sales and customer management
- Credit and risk management
- Ordering and invoicing
- Collections and dispute management
- Payment management

"Pour yourself another cup of coffee, Bob. I'm going to give you a crash course on something called order-to-cash or OTC for short. OTC are the steps from when you set up a customer, take an order, create an invoice, attempt to collect the money, and finally receive the cash in the bank. At each of these steps there are—frankly—opportunities to get it right or to screw it up. We've been screwing up with some of these things and that is why we are . . ."

Bob cut her off. "Don't say a bank!"

"Okay, Bob, then let's just say, that's how we have become . . . more generous. Twenty-plus days more generous. And growing." Carol amused herself at how quickly she felt comfortable ribbing her boss.

In the next few sections, let's look at each of these steps in the OTC process and consider some points of failure as well as best practices.

Sales and Customer Management

If you want your customers to pay you more quickly—or even just to pay you on-time based on your agreement, you need to start at the beginning. A sales team hungry to close deals often has a lot of discretion and can enter all sorts of arrangements on behalf of the company. Pricing and profit margins are almost always closely watched by management, but many seemingly little decisions made by the sales team can greatly affect financial performance downstream and often go unnoticed. This matters because each little decision adds up and further delays the collection of cash. Yet, employees still need to be paid, and the rent is still due. Materials must continue to be purchased, and any plans for expansion or equipment repairs will be affected by the decreasing cash flow.

Start by recognizing that not all customers are equal. Some cost far more to serve than others, not only because of the discounts they negotiate but also because of commercial terms requirements. Segmenting your customer base, you might discover the Pareto principle applies. That is, 80% of your sales are quite possibly generated by 20% of your customers. Do we want to offer all sorts of one-off accommodations to the 80% of customers that likely only generate 20% of sales? Being clear about this and frequently reviewing with your sales team costs to serve customers is key to ensuring they make informed decisions.

Customer ABC wants to award Owens Inc. a big deal, but instead of 45-day payment terms, they are asking for 90-day terms. Take the deal? Push back? It's hard to say without additional detail. Is the margin great enough to offset the carrying cost of an additional 45-day float? ABC is a public company, so we can see that their days payable outstanding is 37 days. On average, ABC is paying their suppliers in 37 days. And they now want to pay us in 90 days? Is this order strategic enough to justify that? Owens also buys from ABC and pays them in 45 days. So now the balance of trade will be off by 45 days? These are real-life, everyday considerations that many organizations gloss over. Winning a big order can be a highly charged event. It's exciting. We don't want to walk away, but do we have support processes in place to help the sales team make good decisions? Do we use segmentation of our customer base to better understand our bargaining positions? If we want to move to a cash culture, we must have well-developed processes and policies in place to guide these decisions.

We also need to train and incentivize our sales teams. Far too often, commissions for sales teams are paid based on the order versus based on the collected revenue. Linking these payments to cash received helps motivate the sales team to get the best price and margin as well as terms that are cash positive. At a minimum, one should have commission/bonus claw-back provisions for seriously late paying or deadbeat customers. We want sales teams to be incentivized to optimize their compensation, generating revenue for the firm. We also want to be sure that revenue converts to cash as quickly as possible.

Sales and Customer Management Best Practices

Some best practices to consider:

- Implement a customer segmentation strategy that includes total cost to serve. This should be an ongoing process, not just a one-time activity. Understanding all the requirements to serve a customer will be helpful in making informed decisions.

- When reviewing pricing and margin on deals, be sure to include the impact of customer terms. In the previous example, the customer wants another 45 days to pay. At a minimum, we'd want to be sure we cover our weighted average cost of capital—in additional margin—for those additional 45 days. If we still want the deal, we need to factor the cash impact into overall financials.

- Link sales compensation to collected cash versus sales orders. Incentivize the sales team to drive deals that support a cash culture.

In summary, no matter how skilled the downstream billing and collections teams have become, ability to quickly collect cash starts with up-front sales and customer management. Linking cash performance to revenue and profit is essential.

Credit and Risk Management

In the previous section, we discussed how to approach customer segmentation and why that helps get a perspective on cost to serve. In this section, I'm going to make an argument for treating everyone alike by applying the same credit review standards to all customers. Many businesses get into trouble by overextending credit to big customers or allowing basic risk management practices to wane because of friendly, long-term relationships. Credit and risk decisions should be carefully guarded, and deviations should be managed by the most senior officers such as the CFO.

It is common to perform credit reviews for new customers, but far too often businesses fail to perform basic ongoing reviews. For example, a customer that always paid on time is now increasingly paying late. Does that trip any sort of alarm? Or in the case of a chronically late-paying customer, do you review your overall exposure? Do you continue to provide services or sell products?

And do you have a firewall between those managing these reviews and those selling and managing the relationships? Credit and risk management must be separate from sales, marketing, and customer management. It's most often part of the CFO's organization.

Credit and Risk Management Best Practices

Some best practices to consider:

- Ensure you have a documented credit review policy that considers onboarding as well as periodic reviews. Create a standard policy first—before considering how it applies to your customers. This takes emotion out of the discussions. There might be very good business decisions to deviate from, but those should be made by a senior officer such as the CFO.

(continued)

(continued)

- Establish a customer risk assessment process that considers exposure to external factors that might affect the customers' ability to fulfill obligations, for example, highly leveraged customers who are more susceptible to inflation or interest rate increases. Consider applying a watch list of those customers you want to more closely monitor their payment performance. Most credit rating agencies also provide updates on sector or regional performance.

- Apply tripwires for customers who start to pay late, conducting a risk review and possibly suspending sales or initiating a service hold.

- For customers who perennially pay late, review the overall cost to serve (and risk exposure). Consider senior executive intervention (CFO-to-CFO or CEO-to-CEO conversations). Be prepared to terminate relationships that might generate sales but do so with significant risk or mounting cost to serve.

- Bring in a third party to audit your credit and risk policies. Review overall credit limits as well as override approval processes.

In summary, credit and risk management is not a one-time activity that happens at the start of a relationship. It must be an ongoing review and triggers need to be in place as the economy shifts or your customer health deteriorates. There must be separation between sales and risk management. Decisions to deviate from credit or risk policies need to be made at the most senior levels of a business.

Ordering and Invoicing

In the "Sales and Customer Management" section, we discussed how commercial terms affect cash performance. There are other requirements customers might present that affect the administrative process of invoicing and collecting. How standard are contracts? Are they written on your paper or the customer's? That means—is it your template or the customer's template? That makes a big difference. If you have hundreds or even thousands of customers, each with their own custom contract, it can become an administrative nightmare to manage the required terms and conditions.

Customers might require additional documentation to accompany an invoice. For example, a customer has a requirement that a purchase order (PO) must be created on their end and the invoice you send them must accurately reflect that PO number. Without it, the customer cannot verify the legitimacy of the invoice and the risk controls they have in place prevent them from paying. This is a common requirement, but perhaps your sales team agreed to a series of complex arrangements, such as the method of taking the order, customized invoice information, special service or delivery considerations, or adherence to one-off contractual arrangements as previously discussed. Suddenly this seemingly simple set of tasks becomes complicated. When we add complexity, we add cost and opportunity for error. It's not just discretionary one-off issues; the overall business operating model over time might increase in complexity.

Let's look at Bob's business. He sells electrical equipment and provides ongoing services as well as warranty protection. Some of these products contain precious metals. To protect against price fluctuations, some of his agreements contain provisions that index the price of those materials to current rates. These constantly changing rates must be factored into the pricing on the invoice. Bob also provides volume discounts and offers rebates when customers hit certain thresholds, which again triggers a series of requirements to keep track of those thresholds and make necessary adjustments. He offers a range of shipping options and passes through those costs, which must be accurately stated and often require additional supporting documentation. Some customers require that he submit invoices via their own internet-based payment portals and others want paper copies sent to each location that ordered from him.

Whether intended or not, billing can become quite complex. Bob built his business providing technically advanced equipment, excellent customer service, and an iron-clad warranty. And although he was careful to keep costs down wherever he could, he neglected to notice how complex he allowed commercial arrangements to become. Similar to reviewing the costs required to serve his customers, Bob would be well served to conduct regular cost-to-sell reviews for business segments. What are the hidden administrative requirements associated with products/services? How do these affect the ability to get a clean invoice out the door quickly?

Ordering and Invoicing Best Practices

Some best practices to consider:

- Don't overthink it. Start by creating a standard template for orders, ensuring your team captures essential information. Make sure they always verify things like correct addresses, PO requirements, and necessary supporting documentation. There are several effective software applications available, but they are only as good as the data you feed them and the process that supports them.

- Measure first-pass yield. This is a fancy way of saying, measure how many invoices get paid on time without any intervention or correction. This will be an eye-opening experience. I've suggested this to CFOs of very large companies who were then shocked to see just how bad things are when measured this way. Remember, every time there is a mistake or information is not presented exactly as your customer requires, it causes delays in getting your cash and drives up your administration costs.

- Perform a review of all the commercial arrangements your team has signed up for. Similar to cost-to-serve reviews for segmented customers, these cost-to-sell reviews not only will help identify the hidden costs but also will expose unnecessary complexity that drives up administrative time and error rates.

In summary, with the best of intentions, we often accommodate customers in all sorts of ways. Many of these accommodations drive up complexity and provide greater opportunity for failure. At the time of the sale, these requirements seem innocuous, but over time and in aggregate, these one-off accommodations erode the quality of ordering and invoicing processes. This then creates confusion with your customers and causes them to delay making payments. A close examination of these processes and of nonstandard accommodations will pay dividends downstream as you attempt to collect your hard-earned money.

Collections and Dispute Management

By this point, I hope I've made the case that all the steps preceding actual collections activity have a profound impact on how much effort is required to collect the money people owe you. In large companies there might be dozens if not hundreds of people dedicated to collections. Day after day they make phone calls and send emails trying to get people to pay. I'll go out on a limb and say that every dollar spent on this activity represents failure upstream.

Think about it. If you have properly vetted your customers, come to agreement on payment terms, did all you could do to deliver your product or service without defect, and provided all the required documentation—to the right location at the right time—you should reasonably expect to be paid according to your agreements without any collections call or intervention.

I'll grant that not all customers act on good faith and might drag their feet in paying, and even the best credit and risk management practices will not prevent all this behavior, but much of the time spent collecting is avoidable. Until we correct the upstream issues, how do we optimize collection activities and make this step in the process as effective and efficient as it can be?

Let's go back to customer segmentation. Recall that we discussed that not all customers are equal. Some customers pay late because they know they can get away with it. They float their payments a few days, maybe a week or more, beyond the agreed-on payment date because there are no repercussions. Maybe they get a tersely written note from time to time, but service is not put on hold and deliveries continue unabated. Do we have an ongoing process to review payment performance? Do collectors have tools at their disposal that can truly change behavior—such as delivery/service holds?

Segmenting customers based on payment performance enables us to tailor collector actions accordingly. Think of this analogy. Monday morning, I start with 20 unread emails. As the day progresses, I get another 30+ emails requiring some action on my part. I can't get to all of them, so I start by answering the easy ones first. As the day and week progress, I keep pushing off the complicated requests. Over time I miss deadlines and add to my workload because the older the request, the more time I must spend to address it. This is a bit like the life of a collector. Each day there are lists of customers who are approaching their payment due period and have not yet paid or have gone past the payment due date. And each unresolved issue stays open until resolved, so this starts to build and build. The older an invoice gets the harder it becomes to collect and there is ever-increasing risk that it will become bad debt.

So, we need a better way to segment these customers and invoices based on payment performance. We need to automate wherever possible the routine tasks, such as reminders and alerts. We also need to align the talent of the team accordingly. Some collectors will be better complex problem-solvers and others are good at processing volume.

There are many great software packages that help manage this process. They provide the structure and governance and help define tasks to be performed. But, like any business process, training and adherence to the process is the key to success. Collections tends to be a high-turnover area of businesses and one where investments in training are often inadequate. Although we'd rather not spend money on collections (if we could just fix the upstream problems), skimping on tools and training will only make matters worse over time.

In addition, most customers are willing and prepared to remit on time, but they withhold the payment because we failed to do something correctly. These are called disputes and they can range from incomplete orders and damaged goods to incorrect purchase order details or lack of required supporting documentation. We need to address and correct or mitigate these disputes before we will be paid. Collectors must first properly understand and accurately record these disputes. We must have a set of dispute codes that is well defined and easy to apply. Then we need resolution processes defined for each code. These become playbooks to resolve problems. It starts with the collector, but to resolve, it will require support from operations (sales, customer service, etc.). The better we are at diagnosing and resolving problems, the quicker we will get our money. The more time we take resolving problems not only prevents us from getting our cash but also drives up cost, as we need to spend more precious time correcting the problem, often pulling folks such as salespeople away from their important primary responsibilities.

It is important that as we resolve each individual dispute, we start to look at the root causes and find ways to prevent similar failures in the future. This is often referred to as having a closed-loop dispute management process.

Collections and Dispute Management Best Practices

Some best practices to consider:

- Segment collections activities based on payment performance of customers. Define actions for each type of late-paying customer and perform ongoing payment performance reviews.

- Allocate portfolios of customers and past due invoices to collectors based on aptitude of collectors.

- Set daily, weekly, and monthly targets for collectors. Try to avoid the trap of dealing with the easiest things first, delaying dealing with more complicated past due invoices. Recall that the older an invoice becomes the more difficult it will be to collect, and it runs greater risk of having to be written off.

- Train collectors how to properly identify disputes and have clear, unambiguous codes for them to use to document. Assign very detailed and prescriptive resolution processes for each code and measure the time it takes to resolve, holding accountable the parties who are responsible at each step of the resolution process.

- Once resolved, look at the root causes of the disputes and initiate a closed-loop process to fix these defects to prevent similar points of failure in the future.

In summary, it would be great if we never had to spend time performing collections activities, but until we get to a state of zero defects on the front end, we will likely need to not only focus on collections but also invest in tools and training to make the processes as efficient and effective as possible.

Payment Management

Your customer has finally committed to pay. You are home free— right? Well . . . how your customer remits payment and how you post the payment or apply the cash represents additional opportunities for complications and cost. Or, if we want to have a glass-half-full attitude, it represents opportunity for businesses to streamline and cut costs.

The 2022 Association of Financial Professionals (AFP) Payments Survey estimates that 92% of businesses in the US still accept checks as a form of payment. This is by far the most expensive way to pay and to receive payment. AFP further estimates that checks can cost the issuer between $2 and $4 per check and the receiver can incur up to an additional $2 in costs associated with processing. These costs start to balloon for large and complex organizations. Despite a steady push toward electronic payments, we seem to be stuck in the past, using a very inefficient form of payment. And, in addition to the cost of payment, there are delays associated with float—or the time it takes for the issuer to send and the receiver to present to their bank and then for the issuer's bank and the receiver's bank to reconcile.

Banks have stepped in, providing a service called lockboxes. These are secure postal locations where the bank receives checks and posts directly to a customer's account. This takes a few steps out of the process, but it doesn't completely solve all the problems associated with checks. Reconciling the payment to individual invoices can still pose problems.

Let's say Owens sells equipment and services to ABC company over a period of a few weeks. And perhaps there are six different invoices involved. ABC decides to consolidate and send one check. Owens still needs to figure out how to apply that payment against each invoice. If everything adds up perfectly, the process is straightforward. But, if ABC short pays for some reason, then trying to decipher how to apply the cash can cause real headaches. It doesn't lessen the time Owens has the cash, but it can drive up administrative costs. Or let's say the opposite occurs and ABC overpays. Owens now needs to figure out if they should issue a refund, apply this to another outstanding invoice, or hold as a credit. All these options—particularly if multiplied by thousands for a mid-size business—create work and expense.

Electronic payments don't eliminate all these problems, but they do dramatically streamline processing.

All the potentially complicated commercial arrangements we discussed earlier once again represent administrative complexity. Rebates, discounts, various financing options complicate the downstream process of applying cash—a tedious and repetitive process. Fortunately, there are several very effective software solutions that use artificial intelligence (AI) and robotic process automation (RPA). These applications can dramatically reduce the administrative time and cost spent in the cash application process. It's these hidden costs that leaders such as Bob often overlook. Further, complexity creeps in when the focus is only on revenue growth. When leaders take a balanced approach and consider total cost to serve as well as the impact on cash flow, commercial arrangements become more intentional.

Payment Management Best Practices

Some best practices to consider:

- Step away from the 1970s and work on eliminating the use and acceptance of checks. The costs to handle and process along with float issues make them a very inefficient form of payment. There are many effective electronic payment options that operate at a fraction of the cost of checks.

- If you still need to accept checks, use lockbox options from banks. Even a small to midsize firm will see a low break-even point when considering the fees banks charge for the service, not to mention enhanced

(continued)

(continued)

security and risk mitigation. If you still need to accept checks, lockbox options make a great deal of sense.

- Investigate options to automate the application process. Cash application is not a value-add process for organizations. Use of RPA and AI not only reduces administrative cost but also it greatly eliminates error rates.

- Up-front commercial arrangements affect all the downstream collection and recording processes. Perhaps we are beating a dead horse, but it's worth repeating. Understanding the cost trade-offs associated with commercial arrangements extended to customers is essential to making intentional business decisions.

In summary, the day has finally come, and you've received some—if not all—of your hard-earned cash. There is still work ahead as you post this cash and reconcile accounts. Electronic payment methods, cash application software, and RPA can decrease administrative costs. But the time and effort that goes into this process is also affected by upstream complexity, the form of the payment, and accompanying documentation.

Summary

"A bank. Hmmm," Bob quietly mumbled.

"What's that?" Carol inquired.

"A bank. I now see what you were saying. I guess we have become a sort of bank to our customers. We chased sales growth and, don't get me wrong, I'm glad we did. We had a record year last year. But we chased growth without considering the impact on cash flow. If we want to sustainably grow our business, we'll need to keep a focus on cash as well as revenue. It was so much easier when we were small. Everyone knew what everyone else was doing. Carol, I hate to admit it, but you were right to say that we took our eyes off the ball."

Knowing not to overplay her hand, Carol didn't respond. The boss was now understanding that Owens chased sales growth, which in itself is not at all bad. But, they did so without considering the trade-offs they were making. They gave away terms to get the sale and they allowed internal processes to get so complex that it was affecting the quality of invoicing and effectiveness of collections.

Bob had been taking several pages of notes and discussed plans with Carol to implement a few new processes and policies. He had always paid close attention to details such as product development, manufacturing, and sales but had not always considered how the OTC processes affected the business. He realized that OTC is not just a back office function. He will need to get his sales and customer support teams on board. The engineer had a plan, and his mood was brightening up. That was until his trusted CFO spoke again.

"Bob, I'm pleased that we had this conversation and that you will help us with some meaningful changes. I was not joking around when I said that we have a real problem with growing receivables. But fixing AR is just the start. If we are serious about focusing on cash, we'll need to address the elephant in the room: inventory."

"Ugh, I was afraid you were going to say that. I know, Carol. Our inventory has been growing out of control. But Yusef and his team are so busy with all the new product launches, I just don't think we can risk messing with that right now."

Carol knew that was not the right answer. There will always be reasons to not examine the problem with inventory, but she also knows her boss. "Baby steps," she thought. "We made good progress on AR today. Perhaps I can get Bob to review accounts payable (AP) next—before we tackle inventory."

"I understand, Bob. In the meantime, why don't we set up time and talk with Jeremy about AP?"

"AP? Let's just do what our customers have been doing to us. We'll just extend payment terms. Viola! Problem solved!" Bob said that with a bit of sarcasm in his voice. He knew that it was not that simple and knew he was being "handled" by his CFO. But when he saw Carol grimace, he realized she did not pick up on the sarcasm. "I mean, that's all we have to do, right?" He said with a wide smile.

"You got me!" Carol recognized his playfulness. "I'll call Jeremy and set things up. Sound good, Boss?"

"It's a deal. And I do so love it when you call me Boss!"

CHAPTER

2

Procure-to-Pay

Procure-to-pay (PTP) are the processes involved in purchasing. PTP receives a great deal more attention than order-to-cash (OTC) in most businesses. Both are important, but PTP tends to get more attention because nothing gets made without materials. And all eyes are on procurement to find ways to source cheaper components. This is the task every day for procurement professionals: find more effective and efficient ways to supply materials to the business. Most procurement departments are always under the gun, dealing with supply chain disruptions, negotiating better pricing, and making sure production lines are not idled for lack of input materials. But the decisions procurement makes every day can greatly affect the balance sheet.

Owens has been in accelerated growth mode, introducing new products and increasing the number of customers they serve. They are also not immune to the many supply chain issues affecting businesses all over. With growth comes pressure to keep up.

The chief procurement officer at Owens is a long distance runner named Jeremy. He has one speed—fast. It's unclear if his job caused him to be this way or if this job was the perfect fit for someone already hyperkinetic.

It's 8 a.m. and Jeremy is already on his third cup of coffee when Bob and Carol walk into his office. Jeremy has a habit of cutting people off mid-sentence and answering questions before the speaker finishes forming them. It's as if every second counts in his world. "Good morning, Jeremy. Carol and I thought we'd stop by and . . ."

Before Bob finished, Jeremy replied, "We got Omega Industries to expedite the shipment this month so we can keep production rates on the G45 at the current level."

"Oh. That's good to hear." Bob had no idea what Jeremy was talking about but guessed he solved a problem before it got to the attention of the president. Bob knew that Jeremy was the right guy for this job. "Carol and I wanted to chat with you about an exercise we went through yesterday. We spent time looking at how we manage our accounts receivable. And we . . ."

Again, before Bob could finish, Jeremy said, "Yes, I heard about that and saw the notes you took on the whiteboard in your conference room. I assumed you'd want to look at procurement in a similar way, so I took the liberty of summarizing PTP steps."

When? Bob wondered when Jeremy did this. He and Carol met until about 4 p.m. yesterday. On top of solving the G45 thing, Jeremy—in his spare time—prepared a review just in case he was asked to do so? On the whiteboard behind his desk, Jeremy had written the following:

- Sourcing strategy
- Supplier and contract management
- Goods receipt and payment management

PTP is sort of like the flipside of OTC, Bob thought. He also thought it best to not suggest more coffee as he and Carol took seats at the small conference table in Jeremy's wildly messy office.

In this chapter, let's look at the PTP process and how cash considerations can play an important role alongside the other objectives procurement teams juggle.

Sourcing Strategy

The life of a sourcing professional is a bit like that of an air traffic controller. Not only do they have to manage routine processes but also they must deal with emergencies that pop up daily. On good days, no one really pays attention to the people "in the tower." Materials arrive just in time to meet production schedules. But things can go wrong, and that was never more apparent than during the recent pandemic. Every household in the country got a crash course in supply chain management when they could not find toilet paper on store shelves. Of course, there were bigger and longer lasting disruptions, but 2020 will go down as the year when we stopped taking TP for granted. And perhaps it was the time most businesses also realized just how critical a role their sourcing teams play in keeping operations running.

But these day-to-day issues can, at times, prevent the organization from stepping back and evaluating the overall strategy. Do we have too much concentration with a single source? If that source or single supplier runs into production or delivery problems, are we now held hostage and our own production is impaired? Or maybe it's the opposite. We spread our spend across too many sources and lose our leverage. These big-picture questions are important but can get sidelined when the key task is "landing all the planes."

Sourcing strategies are also greatly affected by product designs and marketing efforts. Perhaps it's a new ingredient that will be called out in advertising campaigns. "Let's add capsaicin to our pain relief patches."

"Capsaicin?"

"Yes—it's an active ingredient in chili peppers."

"Chili peppers? Like from Mexico?"

"Well, China, Turkey, and Indonesia produce higher quantities at lower prices . . . but, yeah, chili peppers."

So, in addition to sourcing the new ingredient at the lowest cost, the team also needs to consider reliability of the vendor, lead time, and minimum order quantity requirements. Oh, and environmental, social, and governmental (ESG) considerations. Are we trading with firms that embody the values of our company? Do we run the risk of sourcing from a region or country that might be a geopolitical hot spot?

Volumes have been written about how to develop and manage sourcing strategies. It's never quite as simple as it appears on the surface. And, relative to the topic of this book, quite often cash considerations are an afterthought—if considered at all. For example, if we source from low-cost countries in Asia, we can drive down the cost of the material. But this might come with longer lead times, which can drive up the amount of inventory we need on hand, tying up cash. It might also expose us to shifting geopolitical issues that in turn might affect the steady flow of material, again, tying up cash as we sit on partially completed products. This is called *trapped inventory*. So, we might be able to get cheaper chili peppers from China, but in the end, it might make better economic sense—and better cash sense—to pay a bit more and source from Mexico or California.

I've been advising companies for several decades and have found sourcing departments to be highly resistant to change. Getting them to step back and consider strategic approaches is difficult because they juggle so many balls every day. "We just need to get through the next quarter," I frequently hear when trying to advance cash-related enhancements. Then it's "We didn't anticipate the chip shortage, the gridlock in the ports on the West Coast, the fire at a supplier plant in Vietnam, and so on." It's hard to blame them because the planes must safely land, continuing my tortured analogy. But somehow management needs to find ways to help sourcing address bigger-picture, long-term strategies as they manage the day-to-day tasks.

Sourcing Strategy Best Practices

Here are some best practices to follow:

- Leadership needs to provide support to enable sourcing teams to step back from time to time to evaluate their overall strategy and consider trends that are affecting supply chains. Outside consultants can offer this support and provide data and recommendations. (I know this sounds self-serving coming from someone who has spent his career in consulting. I also know that most sourcing groups need this assistance and those who try to do everything internally often fall far behind their peers.)

- Conduct periodic reviews looking at supplier performance. (We will discuss this in greater detail when we cover inventory management.) Consider the impact of supply concentration—too many eggs in one basket? Also consider supply fragmentation—commitments spread too thinly to gain leverage over suppliers.

(continued)

(continued)

- Supply chains are highly integrated organizations. Beneficial long-term relationships need to be balanced. But they also need to be formed using data to support nonemotional negotiations. Again, this is when outside help can be beneficial. There are good sources of benchmark data that can aid in buying and negotiating.

In summary, we will discuss many enhancements in the following sections, but these will be difficult to consider if your organization does not have processes in place to evaluate sourcing strategies. This is an area of the business that gets caught up in day-to-day concerns. There really will never be an ideal time to step back and evaluate. Each month, each quarter a new set of issues will present themselves. Leadership needs to help prioritize strategic reviews that will facilitate enhancements, strengthening sourcing organizations over the long term.

Supplier and Contract Management

Spend cubes, negotiation principles, tail-spend analytics, spend control towers . . . Jeremy can bring a dinner party conversation to a halt when he starts talking about his work. The field of sourcing management has dozens of specialized terms and processes. Hundreds of books have been written and thousands of articles published. Occasionally advances in technology such as artificial intelligence (AI) represent step changes in the field of procurement. But the principles of procurement management have remained mostly constant over the years. The aim of this book, however, is to help organizations adopt a cash culture.

Therefore, we will focus on some of the things within sourcing control that have impact on cash.

Payment terms are likely what most people think of but other things such as payment frequency, payment triggers, and terms adherence are also quite important. Minimum order quantity and lead time requirements directly affect how much inventory one must hold, and that consumes cash. Incoterms are globally accepted protocols that govern responsibilities and ownership while goods are in transit. These terms also can affect when inventory ownership hits your books, as well as when you are responsible for insurance and taxes. Again, these things can affect cash flow.

Our focus will be on some of these cash-related drivers. We'll cover some of that review in this section, as well as in sections that discuss goods receipt and inventory management. And if this book ever becomes popular enough to become a drinking game, you should know up front that the word *segmentation*, if used as the trigger word, might transport you back to your college days. Just as we used segmentation for customers and segmentation for receivables, we will use segmentation for suppliers and for spend. Hint: you will likely tip your glass again during the chapter on inventory.

Before we get into discussing options to pursue commercial arrangements that—as a buyer—are beneficial to your company, we need to determine how much power we have.

Let's say it's a lazy Saturday afternoon and you decide to head over to an antiques fair in the parking lot of a local junior high. You see an emerald and blue Persian rug that would look perfect in your dining room. The price is quite a bit higher than you think you should spend right now, not to mention that even if someone helps you tie it to the roof of your car, it will be too big and too heavy for you to unload and place in your home. Ah, but details. It really is perfect, you think.

Now, the clearly seasoned owner of the stand selling the rug notices that you've been looking at it for several minutes and she heard you mumble under your breath, "Oh, wow." She approaches. You gather your resolve. The rug will be yours if you can strike the right price. Then the two of you are figuratively transported away from the junior high parking lot to the souks of Marrakech and you engage in the centuries-old practice of rug bartering. After several minutes of back-and-forth, frowns, and grimaces by you and the seller, you win. You get her to agree to a price you feel good about. Being the master trader she is, the seller looks pained as you complete your payment. Only until you are out of sight does she smile widely because she also won, getting far more for the old flea-bitten rug than she guessed when she hauled it out to the lot that morning.

How to get it from the car to the house? There are several neighbor kids who are always looking for quick spending cash. You call one of your neighbors. "Hi, Ellen, would Joel like to earn $10? I need help moving a rug I just bought." Joel would. That problem is solved. One stop at Mega-Lo-Mart on the way home to get a $49 rug pad, then you will soon have that majestic antique (buyer's term for old, flea-bitten) rug grace your dining room floor.

This vignette illustrates the polarity of buying power. At one end, you plop down $49 for a rug pad at Mega-Lo-Mart because you are one of millions of customers. You—as an individual— have no bargaining power. The price presented by Mega-Lo is the price you pay. At the other pole, Joel takes your offer of $10. If the kid wanted more, you know plenty of other teenagers in your neighborhood looking for pizza money. You have complete control over the price you pay, and Joel gets $10 and not a penny more. And of course, there is the haggling over the rug at the antiques fair. You have some negotiating power and you drove the price down to fit your budget. The seller had power too as you had no data at your disposal about the cost of similar rugs sold that day at the fair. She wanted to off-load the rug, so she didn't have to haul it back to her storage unit and you, well, you already pictured Thanksgiving dinner with that rug in place. You allowed emotions to influence the negotiation.

In a similar way, companies operate along this continuum with every buy-sell transaction. Some things like tax or debt payments are non-negotiable (yes, good lawyers might be able to help with both, but let's assume the terms are not up for negotiation), and other things you buy enough of or have enough buying power to set your terms. Take it or leave it. Then there is all the stuff in the middle. The key is to build a segmentation model that defines the conditions that determine these positions. Is the material or service you are buying so specific that you can't substitute for something else? Are there multiple providers or sources? What is the changeover cost of switching to another supplier? If you deviate from the terms, say you pay late, are there penalties? Are their risks to your business if you can't get the material or service on time?

These are just some examples of conditions that determine the following categories:

- **Seller must take it or leave it:** I have power. (There are plenty of other kids who could step in for Joel and the service of carrying a heavy rug is not very specialized.)
- **Negotiate:** I have some power. (But if I'm determined to get that specific rug, I might have to make some concessions.)
- **Buyer must take it as is:** I have no power. (Mega-Lo-Mart doesn't care if I thought $39 was a better price. I could drive across town to Dollar Bush, but I need the pad now so $49 is in the till at Mega-Lo.)

An effective segmentation model, at a minimum, should consider criticality, the nature of the market, and switching considerations.

- **Criticality:** How critical is the material or service being provided? During the pandemic we found snack alternatives to empty tortilla chip shelves . . . but toilet paper? Some things we really can't live without. In addition, is the material or service rather specialized or is it more of a commodity? Perhaps we preferred the extra soft toilet paper we grew accustomed to during the halcyon days before the pandemic. But rather than do without, we found ways to live with the see-through single ply.

- **Market:** How many alternative vendors do we have to choose from? Are we restricted to certain areas to source from? For example, some minerals and precious metals come from only a small number of locations and vendors. If these are critical to our business, then we have a criticality factor and a market restriction. And, how big a buyer are we for this product or service? In our rug example, we buy one rug pad from a giant store so there is no way we can negotiate with Mega-Lo. But there are a lot of neighbor kids we can find to help us, so the price we set is the price we will get.

- **Switching:** Setting up new vendors might be quite difficult and expensive. The issue Jeremy was working on with Omega Industries involved special plastic components that required a custom die that Omega had to make just for Owens. If Jeremy wants to switch vendors, he will need to invest in creating new dies. Not only are there cost considerations but also there are time impacts. Even if it made economic sense for Jeremy to commission new dies, the time to ramp up production with a new vendor might be quite disruptive to operations. But in the case of office products, for example, switching vendors might be a breeze.

To properly evaluate how much negotiating room we have with vendors and how to enter the most favorable contracts, we need to segment our sourcing requirements and vendors.

This segmentation applies not only to the price you pay but also to the commercial arrangements, such as minimum order quantities, service levels, and payment terms. And, sadly, payment terms are commonly the last thing discussed during the purchasing process. Price, quantity, as well as other specifications are often settled on before payment terms are discussed. Far too often businesses either take a one-size-fits-all approach with, say, standard terms of 45 days or find themselves accepting a blizzard of terms that vendors put forward. Applying the logic of segmentation and understanding buying power is the start of an effective buying process, but then one needs to consider the prevailing terms for that specific commodity. Benchmark data exists that can aid buyers in determining optimal payment terms.

The issue with blanket terms is that many categories, such as professional services/consulting, are accustomed to accepting terms greater than our 45-day example. It's perfectly fine to have some sort of base-level standard or a not-to-go-below term, but to get the most out of the sourcing process, differentiated terms need to be considered.

We'll discuss the payment clock, payment frequency, and payment type in the next section. These are important levers, in addition to payment terms, that need to be part of an overall strategy. It's so much more effective to start with segmentation to understand our relative power in the buying process. Based on the segment these might be take-it-or-leave-it conversations with vendors. For others, such as tax authorities, they call the shots, and then for the majority in the middle we build negotiation strategies using this information to our advantage.

Supplier and Contract Management Best Practices

Some best practices to consider:

- Before you consider changing commercial terms, segment your vendors/spend into categories that consider factors such as criticality, market conditions, and impact of switching. Then evaluate your position of power in the trade. Broadly speaking, you will end up with three categories: you can dictate terms, the vendor can dictate terms, or there is room for negotiation.

- Payment and other commercial terms should be on the table at the same time as pricing. It's important to get full leverage—where possible.

- In your segmentation assessment you might want to consider other factors such as the overall health of the supply chain. Making a short-term gain only to face a longer-term unstable supply base is not wise. You might want to evaluate your suppliers using ESG criteria. Do your partners reflect your values? Will your association with the supplier enhance your social capital? Are there geopolitical concerns associated with trade in a certain region, causing vulnerability in the near future?

- Use available data sources. This is where consultants can add real value because they have data and models readily available, so you don't spend precious time and energy trying to reinvent the wheel.

> - Conduct periodic reviews of suppliers, considering quality, responsiveness, and ease of doing business. Assess your ongoing balance of trade (if applicable). That's when you buy from and sell to the same entity.

In summary, if we want to create a cash culture we must look not only at lowest price. Factors such as where material is sourced from that might affect lead times, minimum order quantity requirements, and payment terms need to be weighed.

Goods Receipt and Payment Management

After a couple of hours in Jeremy's cramped office, Carol suggested they stretch their legs and get some fresh air. Bob loved the idea. Once outside, Jeremy pointed to the parking lot behind the main loading docks. "You know, when I first started with Owens I could walk out here and tell you the day of the month without looking at a calendar," Jeremy exclaimed as he pointed to the area where semitrailers wait to be unloaded.

"Is that right?" Bob reflexively said as he read several messages on his phone.

"Well, I put a stop to that right away!" Jeremy was beaming with pride.

Bob had looked up from his phone, wondering what on earth that meant, but took the bait anyway. "What? What did you do?"

"Purchase orders! I made sure we had 100% compliance issuing and enforcing purchase orders."

Bob looked at his overly enthusiastic head of purchasing and wondered if that small, crowded office was affecting Jeremy somehow. "Jeremy, what on earth are you talking about? You can tell the time of the month by looking at our parking lot? And what's all this about purchase orders? You've lost me." Carol smiled. She interacts with Jeremy more often and has become accustomed to his nonlinear way of talking.

Jeremy started to speak a bit louder and slower—the way one explains a 100-button remote control to a grandparent. "When I started at Owens, I noticed that the last few days of every month this parking lot was filled with semitrailers. Because we had been lax at issuing and enforcing purchase orders, our vendors sent material early so they could get the inventory off their books before the first of the month. Not only were we taking inventory too early—onto our books—we were also paying them faster than we needed. Let's go back inside and I'll explain."

A great deal of thought and work goes into up-front negotiations with suppliers, but the back end—how material is received and, frankly, when it is received also affects the balance sheet. Ideally, we want materials to arrive at the right place, at the right time, and in the correct quantity. And only then do we want the payment clock to start. Jeremy noticed, when he started at Owens, that some suppliers realized that Owens was not all that disciplined in this area, so they started to advance ship. They would send orders a few days or even a few weeks in advance of the order receipt date. The suppliers were able to get the inventory off their books, but Owens was taking on inventory prematurely. Receiving managers at Owens were not that concerned because their primary concern was managing a metric called on time—in full (OTIF). They knew that production lines were idled if their materials did not arrive on time and in full. So, advance receiving gave a nice buffer and kept things moving smoothly. But, like everything in supply management, there are trade-offs. (We'll explore scheduling in more detail in Chapter 3.)

Jeremy also noticed that Owens did not always require the use of purchase orders (POs) or enforce their terms. POs are agreements that specify quantities, pricing, timing, delivery instructions, commercial terms, and so on. Although master contracts provide blanket contract terms, purchase orders enable buyers to communicate specifications with suppliers. Jeremy noticed that suppliers were advance shipping, so he cracked down on the enforcement of purchase orders. Although the example used here is for materials, POs are also effective tools for procurement and acceptance of services as well.

Carol started this discovery journey when she told Bob that Owens was becoming a bank. Owens was floating customers, allowing them to pay quite late. But Owens was also prematurely paying their suppliers. This too adds a bit of financing to the supply base. As we discussed, there might be great reasons to provide additional financial support to suppliers, but the key—as with all these processes—is to make intentional decisions.

One leading cause of early payments is prematurely starting the payment clock. For example, if the payment terms are 60 days, then 60 days after the clock starts, the payment is due to the vendor. Ideally, the payment clock starts when the good or service is received at the planned time. If the PO calls for the material to arrive on the 12th, then that's the earliest the clock should start. If, however, material arrives on the 8th, the clock should not start four days prematurely. Often there are data and systems limitations implementing this type of practice because it requires planned for and actual receipt data to be aligned. The best next proxy is receipt of the invoice. The worst and sadly most common way to start the clock is based on the invoice date.

A vendor sends the invoice (whether electronically or through snail mail) and the date on the invoice triggers the clock. The problem with this is that the invoice could be delayed, could go to the wrong place, might contain incorrect information, and so on. It can also be manipulated. If I receive an invoice on the 20th but the date is the 5th and I start my payment clock based on the 5th, then I've lost 15 days to plan for and make that payment. At a minimum, we should always specify the receipt of the invoice as the start of the clock. This places the burden on the vendor to comply with PO terms and to ensure timely and accurate issuance of invoices.

Let's also consider payment frequency. Ideally, we never want to pull payments forward and always pay in arrears. If something is due on a Saturday or a bank holiday, it should be paid on the next business day. It is also quite common to inform vendors that we only do two payment runs a month—say the 1st and the 15th. If the invoice arrives on the 3rd of May and has 60-day terms and we only pay twice a month, the payment will be remitted on July 15th. This provides additional conservation of cash and makes forecasting of disbursements easier. However, there are always exceptions, such as taxes, rent, and utilities, which tend to be non-negotiable.

The mode of payment is also a factor of consideration. ACH and wire payments are the most efficient modes. They enable a payment to be received on a precise date. If we negotiate extended payment terms, and implement a twice-monthly remittance date, then we need to be accurate with the payment dates. Vendors can accept longer terms if they can accurately forecast the receipt of the cash. We can implement policies beneficial to our business but must always consider the impact on our supply base. They need to know that if we say we will pay on the 15th, we do pay on that date. Checks are troublesome because of the float and the administrative cost of handling.

There are several other fintech solutions available to help manage payments. I'll comment on one that is quite mature and very straightforward. There are payment vehicles banks offer called *vCards*. Many might be familiar with a pCard or a purchasing card. pCards are actual credit cards that are used by purchasing—often with limitations on the types of things that can be bought. A vCard is a virtual version of that. Purchasing can run through payments using an assigned account number. Not only does this provide the float of 30+ days common to credit cards, it also often provides cashback rebates. This works best with indirect suppliers (think office supplies) or smaller purchases. Banks can run an analysis and show you which of your vendors already accepts payment via credit card—these become no-brainer switches.

Goods Receipt and Payment Management Best Practices

Some best practices to consider:

- Taking control of the receipt of a good or service is critically important when creating a cash culture. Materials should arrive at the right time, in the right location, and according to specifications. Ownership should not transfer in advance.

- POs provide an additional layer of documentation. Buyers can specify timing, quantities, pricing, delivery instructions, and so on. In addition to requiring POs, make sure that there is strict adherence to the specifications of the PO. Until the vendor complies, payment should be withheld.

- The payment clock starts the payment process. The most common—and worst—trigger is based on the invoice date. More mature businesses have required that the clock starts, at a minimum, on the receipt of

(continued)

(*continued*)

    the invoice. Or, ideally, the later of the receipt of the invoice or the receipt of the good or service on or after the planned receipt date.

- When possible, payments should be made in arrears. Do not pull forward on weekends or holidays. A leading practice in the US is to remit twice monthly in arrears. Like all adjustments to commercial terms this requires a segmentation analysis. There are some spend categories such as tax and utility payments in which we still might need to remit slightly in advance of the due date. But most spend can be remitted in arrears.

- There are several fintech platforms assisting with remittance that are worth investigating. pCards and vCards are quite common and easy to implement and might be a good addition to payment methods

- The key to any good relationship is open communication and following through with commitments. This most certainly applies to supplier relationships. If we want to extend commercial terms, adjust the payment clock and set up payment in arrears, then we must remit accordingly and not further delay or hold back payments. Our ability to negotiate more favorable terms is based on our good reputation. That does not mean we need to be more generous than our competitors, just that we need to do as we say.

Much effort goes into selecting suppliers and setting up favorable commercial relationships. The way these materials or services are received and the way we then remit payment can have a big impact on cash. We don't want inventory on our books too soon nor do we want to pay before we must. We should consider benchmark data that helps determine the reasonable payment terms for a category of spend, and we should implement leading practices that many of our competitors likely have already established That said, we acknowledge that we need healthy relationships with our supply partners and after we conclude negotiations, we should be true to our word and remit on time.

Summary

In most companies, the procurement team plays a critical role. They are tasked with sourcing materials to meet design and engineering specifications. They not only need to get the best price possible but also they need to ensure the materials arrive on time to meet manufacturing schedules. At the end of the day, no one starts cheering and clapping for the procurement team because everything operated as planned. "Wow! Great job! We had just what we needed to follow our build plan today. Thank you, procurement team!" But when something goes wrong . . .

There is so much pressure to get things right that it's somewhat forgivable if the procurement team doesn't always see the other trade-offs that affect cash. Minimum order quantities, lead times, delivery schedules all affect how much cash is tied up in inventory. Payment terms and payment frequency also affect cash balances because they dictate how quickly we must part with it.

"If you want extended payment terms, expect higher prices." That is a very common refrain from procurement teams. And can you blame them? They are juggling so many balls, and as said, they are always the bad guys when things go wrong and never the heroes when everything goes as planned. But there are benchmarks and data as well as segmentation and risk models that can aid with these trade-off discussions. If we want our procurement teams to focus on cash in addition to quality, service levels, price, and now ESG concerns, we need to provide them with the tools and support to do so.

And we need to walk by their offices more often and thank them for "safely landing those planes" every day.

Bob and Carol exchanged glances. It was time to leave their purchasing all-star, Jeremy, and let him get back to his work. As they walked down the hall, Carol said, "You know, Bob, we have a lot we can do to improve our order to cash and procure-to-pay processes and no doubt that will yield strong results. But . . ." Apparently Jeremy was rubbing off on Bob, for he cut off Carol.

"But we are sitting on a ton of inventory and that is tying up precious cash."

"Bob, we might just make a finance executive out of you after all!" This was possibly pushing the limits of familiarity with the president, but Bob chuckled, so it must have been well received. They agreed to set up meetings next week with Yusef, VP of operations.

3

Forecast to Fulfill

Yusef's assistant sits outside a mostly empty office day after day. No calls ever come through for him because everyone calls his cell phone. Yusef is a roamer. As VP of operations at Owens, he takes it on himself to be where the action is. There is a dented-up desk next to a second-hand whiteboard in a corner of the main factory floor that serves as his real office. If Bob is the soul of the company, Yusef is the life force. He is employee number 107.

Bob and Yusef are dear friends in addition to work colleagues, and there is no one Bob trusts more. The board has been pressing Bob to commit to naming Yusef his successor, yet Bob is reluctant to do that. It's not that Bob doesn't think Yusef could do a great job as president; it's that he worries it would kill the man. As it is, Yusef is in the plants 12+ hours a day and comes in on the weekends as well. Bob can't recall when Yusef last took a vacation of more than three days. He is the epitome of a workaholic.

Always dressed in khakis and a short-sleeve shirt with the Owens logo, Yusef quite literally gets his hands dirty in the tasks of operating the main factory. So, when Bob passed Yusef's usually empty office to see him in suit and tie sitting at his desk, it stopped him in his tracks.

"Funeral?" Bob blurted out.

"What?" a confused Yusef replied.

Bob continued. "Oh! Are we finally getting rid of you? You must have a job interview? Hey, man, I'll write a great reference for you. You know, I'll make up all sorts of things like you are sensitive, caring, and have perfected a wonderful work-life balance."

"I am too funny," Bob thought.

"Ha. Ha. Ha. Very funny, Boss." Yusef always calls Bob *Boss*. They live a block from each other, their wives are close friends, and their kids went to school together. Yet, Yusef only rarely calls Bob by his name. The most recent time was at a Rotary lunch where he welcomed his dear friend "Bob" to the dais and both men exchanged glances like "that was kind of weird."

"I'm just dressing for my next job, Boss. Yours!" Yusef upped the ante with the playful banter. He continued, "I hear you are making quite a mess of things, Boss. Going around, second-guessing what everyone does. My team tells me that it's only a matter of time before you want to tell your operations team how to do their jobs."

"Listen here, my friend. I was operating this plant before you could tie your shoes! Darn right I think I know a thing or two about operations," Bob said with a completely playful tone.

"Ah, yes, but that's when folks still used steam engines and an abacus." As Yusef said this, he slightly feared he might be pushing things a bit too far. He and Bob have an excellent relationship that is built on mutual trust and admiration. Yusef looks up to Bob and considers him his mentor in addition to his friend. Thankfully, Bob's response was hearty laughter.

"All kidding aside, Boss, I have heard that you are making the rounds. It's about cash, I believe. Trying to get a better handle on how we manage our precious operating cash. Is that right?"

"Exactly." Bob replied. "As I talk with folks across the business, I am realizing how complicated our little company has become. I thought I knew about everything that is going on. But I'm coming to realize that so many people, through their daily routines, make decisions—often quite logical—but they make decisions that affect our balance sheet. Our cash flow. Of course, Yusef, you know that our biggest investment in working capital/cash is in inventory. So, yes, my friend, it really was only a matter of time for me to come down and find out just how big a mess you've made," Bob winked.

"Boss, have a seat. I've been expecting you."

Yusef brought to the table what looked like a model of a long boat. But this boat didn't seem to have a stern, instead there were two bows. Further, there were 8 or 10 oars, but half were pointed in one direction and the other half in the opposite direction. It was a very odd-looking craft. Bob knew that Yusef is a boating enthusiast, having been on the rowing team in college.

"Now I understand why your crew never beat ours," Bob said, stoking up the rivalry between their alma maters.

"Boss, this is the good ship Owens. If you want to know why we have so much inventory, you need to understand how our boat works."

Looking more closely at the model, Bob could see that Yusef labeled each oar. One was marketing, another finance, and so on. Then he looked at the whiteboard behind Yusef and saw that his old friend had written this:

- Procurement
- Sales
- Marketing/engineering

- Logistics/warehousing
- Finance
- Production

Yusef resumed. "This boat is much like our business. Each oar represents a different function. And each oar, if not synchronized, just slams against the water, splashing about and the boat spins and flails. This is also the way we manage inventory. Each function has their own interests and goals, and if not synchronized, our inventory doubles like it has these past few years. Boss, I wish it was as simple as 'beat up old Yusef' and you'll get inventory under control, but I represent just one or two of the oars. To solve for this, we need to look at each oar and get them rowing in the same direction."

Let's walk through some examples.

Procurement

As we discussed, procurement teams are most often focused on negotiating the lowest price. This, however, can come at the cost of higher inventory if there are long lead times, erratic availability, and large minimum order requirements. In addition, many procurement teams are organized in a way that discourages supplier consolidation and encourages either transactional relationships or those that are far too cozy. In a transactional relationship, there is little incentive for the supplier to creatively engage in trade-off discussions that can ultimately bring costs down, service levels up, and just-in-time inventory. Although too-cozy relationships often don't use current data to challenge the status quo, and the old way of doing business reigns.

Procurement Best Practices

Some best practices to consider:

- Create, maintain, and regularly review supplier score-cards, measuring performance in areas such as quality, on time—in full, purchase price variance, and dispute resolution processes. Re-source materials from unreliable vendors and offer incentives and rewards to vendors who exceed expectations.

- Foster collaboration with suppliers. Review opportunities to concentrate purchase when the risk of disruption is low, gaining pricing and service advantages. Conversely, adjust concentration if disruption risk is high. It's important to use market and benchmark data to strike the right balance between self-interest and a mutually beneficial relationship.

- Calculate the total cost of ownership/relationship with suppliers. Ensure you consider surcharges, penalties, order flexibility, packaging, labeling, and transportation costs.

- Initiate a process to routinely review supply constraints, ensuring the root causes are identified and documented. All too often, the first reaction to constraints is to order more material.

- Review and update safety stock formulas on a regular basis. Underlying drivers and conditions change over time, which might positively or negatively affect formula assumptions.

Sales

We most often incentivize our sales teams to chase every deal, whether or not it is truly in our best economic interests. This results in commercial terms being a bit of an afterthought. Payment, billing, and contract terms can affect accounts receivable. And service level and delivery commitments can truly affect the amount of inventory we must carry. Additionally, it's often quite hard for sales teams to agree to paring down the catalog of offerings. Slow-moving stock keeping units (SKUs) might be kept on the books years after justified demand has waned. And new features and SKUs might be introduced without proper cost-to-serve analysis because our sales team advises us that the bigger deal is dependent on them. These might be quite legitimate arguments, but unless evaluated for their true merits, this can quickly get out of control and inventory can balloon. As we discussed, not all sales deals nor all customers are of equal value, yet the decisions made can have equal if not outsized impact on inventory.

Sales Best Practices

Some best practices to consider:

- Implement and follow a sales and operations planning process that is well documented and that is led by combined leadership team (sales, marketing, finance, operations. etc.). Use this process to reconcile sales (demand) forecasts with production capacity and supply availability.

- Coalesce on one set of numbers (data) used by sales and marketing, finance, and operations planning.

- Document and follow a formal process to identify and resolve changing business conditions that will negatively affect forecasts. Factor into considerations the total cost to serve. (Example: A long-time client continues to change orders within the agreed-on "lockdown period." This results in both excess inventory as well as increased production costs. Although we love to take more orders, we need to do so with insight into total costs.)

- Align goals and performance targets to promote balanced behaviors. If we incentivize sales teams only by revenue and further don't consider forecast accuracy, we take away an important and powerful signal in the planning process.

Marketing/Engineering

Imagine a new product introduction in which the marketing team tried to dampen enthusiasm and downplay expectations. It doesn't happen. Marketing almost always is highly optimistic, which can lead to unrealistic inventory buildup—particularly if marketing and sales are not in alignment. Setting aside what might be unrealistic projections, how the product specifications are created can significantly affect required inventory—particularly if it's hard to source and has erratic supply availability. All too often, specifications are made without advance consultation with the purchasing team, who then must scramble to find sources. (Recall the capsaicin pepper discussion in Chapter 2?)

Design updates from engineering might leave a lot of raw material obsolete if they don't manage the cut-in process effectively. For example, a new fastener is specified by engineering. Owens currently has six months' supply of the old fasteners. The cut-in process is 30 days. Unless there is another use for the old fastener, Owens is now stuck with five months' supply of inventory of a part with no demand. Warranty requirements can also overforecast the number of spare parts that must be on hand for after-sales service support.

Marketing/Engineering Best Practices

Some best practices to consider:

- Implement and follow a formal SKU review process, identifying products with waning or no demand as well as those that have become unprofitable. Follow a disposition process for these products and materials, paying close attention to possible expiry windows. Remove these SKUs from product offerings.

- In a similar way, conduct formal reviews of new SKU introductions and ensure the demand projections have been properly vetted. Often these new SKUs are variations of or minor enhancements to existing products, but not all these variations and options are advisable when considering the total cost impact (additional inventory, additional production steps, portfolio complexity, etc.).

- Follow a documented phase-in process for new SKUs and engineering changes. Pay close attention to existing SKUs on hand, and wherever possible ensure the cut-in process absorbs existing materials before purchasing new materials.

- Review on an annual basis engineering hours charged. Most activity, design enhancements, changes, and so on are effective. But as Elon Musk has famously noted, the most common mistake made is to optimize something that should not exist.

Logistics/Warehousing

Having the right material at the right place and at the right time is a big part of the aim for an optimized logistics function. But, at what cost and how do we define things like "right time?" If right time means a 95% service level, that will require a lot more inventory on hand than say an 80% service level. Is there room for differentiated service levels? Multi-echelon planning is a concept that considers stocking strategies with differentiated service levels across the network. For example, some material might be centrally held and then sent out to plants with a three- to five-day lead time. Other materials need to be stocked on site or at distribution facilities that enable a shorter lead time. We will discuss logistics strategies in greater detail in Chapter 4.

Finance

Finance teams never send mixed signals—right? Not intentionally, of course, but finance can be a partner in crime in driving up inventory. For example, plant managers might be measured on asset absorption costs. This incentivizes them to run assets (machines) longer and produce bigger batch sizes, so the cost of the expensive asset is absorbed across more material/inventory. This works if it matches demand, but if it gets ahead of demand, you just end up creating more inventory that remains on your books, offsetting the accounting benefits. In Chapter 6, we will explore several ways that finance can avoid sending mixed signals and can play a more helpful role in managing inventory.

Production

Who owns inventory? This is a question I love to ask senior leaders. Some might answer that material managers own it. Others might say plant managers, division presidents, or supply chain operations. The reality is that although there might be someone or some group designated to "own" inventory, that doesn't always mean they can control the amount they own. By the time the material arrives at the plant, many others have been involved. As we've discussed in the preceding sections, the marketing team launches a new product feature and predicts big sales. To hit those high sales projections, the sales team agrees to commercial terms that make it more favorable to customers—perhaps guaranteed service level of two-day delivery and lower minimum order requirements. This new product required new machines and reconfiguration of existing equipment. Engineering provided new specifications, which meant some older parts are now obsolete. Finance modeled the absorption costs associated with the new product, thus leading to long run times and big batch sizes at the plant. So, who again owns inventory? Each of these functions—and more—contribute to the amount of inventory building up.

No doubt, production plays a key role. If they don't follow planning schedules or if they create inefficiencies in production throughput, they also drive up inventory. In Chapter 5, we walk through a day in the life of a plant manager and we'll look at ways to ensure operations optimizes the processes under its control.

Summary

Although Yusef does play a critical role in managing inventory, most all other parts of the business also play a contributing role. His model of a boat with oars all rowing in different directions is a very useful reminder that in most businesses competing priorities arise, often to the detriment of the balance sheet.

In the next four chapters, we will look at this in more detail:

- Logistics
- Production
- Finance
- Metrics

"Yusef, if I didn't know you better, I'd swear you are trying to pass the buck."

"Boss, because I do know you quite well, I know that you understand the buck always stops with you." Yusef flashed his million-dollar smile at Bob and continued. "I can help you get our growing inventory under control but to do that, we need to understand the root causes. And, once we do, we'll need to get all the oars in our boat rowing in the same direction. That's why I'm wearing this boss-man suit today. I'm ready to step up and help you run the company—not in silos—but in a coordinated way."

Bob—not one to normally be caught off guard—was. "Step up and help run the company? I would love that Yusef. You know that all the jokes and ribbing aside, I greatly value your thoughts and opinions. And the suit? It's a bit more theatrical than we usually go for here, but I still love it."

Yusef smiled broadly, reached out, and shook Bob's hand. "Tomorrow, let's do a deep dive into logistics. The decisions we make there have real impact across our supply chain. I'll work with Mr. Harris to prep for that."

Yusef and Bob got up from the table and walked into the hall. Chris, Yusef's assistant, walked up to the men and said, "Yusef, I confirmed your reservation for two at Le Jardin at seven tonight. The table on the terrace was available so I booked that."

Bob stopped walking. "Wait a minute! Le Jardin table for two? You didn't wear that suit today because you want to impress me, did you?" he said with his booming, "I'm the president" voice.

With a sheepish reply and a devilish grin, "It my wedding anniversary. I'm taking Nadine to dinner. I mean, you know, we were on a roll, Boss, and it sounded so good. And, uhm, well, you know, you got choked up—remember?"

"I certainly remember to never play poker with you, Yusef! You two-bit hustler!" Chris looked confused as he watched the two men walk away, continuing to insult each other.

4

Logistics

"How was your fancy dinner?" Bob asked Yusef as he walked into the conference room next to his office.

Yusef replied, "Nadine loved it. Her friends have been egging her on for months to go there. But you know me, I'm quite happy with a simple burger and some fries. I don't need fancy."

"Is that right? You see yourself as a real man of the people? Just an ordinary Joe? . . . Say, how's that 40-foot sailboat of yours? Mister 'man of the people'?" Bob was wound up and ready to go. Yusef just smiled and ignored the taunts from his boss.

"Gentlemen, good morning. I hope I've not been keeping you."

"Not at all, Mr. Harris. Yusef was just telling me about how in touch he is with the common man."

Owens is a first-name basis company. Everyone calls Bob Moore, Bob. Well, everyone except Yusef, who calls him Boss. There is, however, Mr. Ted Harris who is universally addressed as Mr. Harris. Bob would never think of greeting him as simply

Jamal. Mr. Harris has been at Owens for 100 years—or so the folklore goes. He was there when Bob started, and he was Yusef's first manager. The folks in HR probably know how old he is, but no one would dare ask Mr. Harris his age.

He has held many different jobs at Owens, and for the last year or so Yusef has asked Mr. Harris to help him sort out what has become an increasingly complex logistics process. He joined Yusef and Bob that morning to explore how this issue affects inventory and therefore cash flow.

Broadly speaking there are three categories of logistics:

- Procurement logistics (inbound from suppliers)
- Production logistics (materials management)
- Sales logistics (outbound to customers)

We covered many aspects of procured logistics in Chapter 2, and when we examine a day in the life of a plant manager (Chapter 5), we will look at materials management. For now, we will consider the process of packaging and delivering products to customers.

Packaging and Delivering Products to Customers

This is by no means a static field of study. Customers constantly change their requirements, the costs associated with transportation fluctuate on a regular basis, and innovation both provides new opportunities and disrupts the status quo. The global pandemic also altered almost everything about how customers receive products and how companies must respond.

Stuck at home, consumers turned to e-commerce for just about every need. For example, let's say you run out of liquid dish soap. Rather than driving over to a grocery to buy it there, you now might place a one-click order on your phone and expect the single bottle to arrive at your door the next day.

Now, let's consider the ripple effect this has on the supply chain. In the old model, a manufacturer of dish soap would fill entire trucks with pallets of the product. They would send these off to distribution centers operated by the grocers, who would unpack and send entire cases of soap to stores. More unpacking and the soap eventually goes on shelves. Then, the consumer is responsible for going to those stores, buying, and transporting the soap back to his home.

Now, the manufacturer might need to find a way to package individual bottles of dish soap, sending them one at a time directly to the end consumer's home. Instead of sending entire truck loads to dozens of locations, they now send a bottle or two at a time to more than 120 million household locations . . . and that's just in the US! In the old model, the consumer took responsibility for the last mile of logistics, bringing goods from stores (physical locations) to their homes. In the new model, the marketer might now have responsibility for the last mile, directly to the consumer's doorstep.

This is just one change that is occurring, affecting logistics. Other market challenges include the following:

- Rising costs of fuel, which increases the cost of transportation
- Labor shortages
- Increasingly global supply chains
- Inflation
- Regulatory changes associated with climate objectives
- Consumer preference volatility

These and many other challenges not only drive up costs for businesses but also drive up inventory. Yusef poured himself a cup of tea and sat across from Bob and Mr. Harris. "Boss, do you know what goes on here?"

"That's a setup. Of course, I think I know what goes on in the company I lead, but I'm sure you are going to tell me otherwise," Bob replied.

"I mean no disrespect, Boss, but this business has become quite complex. No one should expect a president to know everything. Or let me put it a different way. No one person can possibly know all the things going on in a business such as ours. You started this series of internal discussions because you want to get better control of cash. When businesses grow and become more complex, they start to burn through cash faster and its harder and harder to figure out how to address that." Yusef spoke quietly, almost reverently. He and Bob like to tease back-and-forth, but they also can get quite serious and focused and especially so in front of others. This is one of the traits Bob most loves about his trusted deputy.

"It's crazy, Yusef. I see the numbers and the charts, and it just stares me in the face. We have grown inventory greater than sales year after year. If we were also grabbing market share or even improving customer service levels, I might be inclined to accept our increasing investment in inventory, but it's just not the case. We grew sales last year at about the same pace as the market. I don't see any big market share gain."

"Yep. And, Boss, our stock-outs and missed sales have gotten worse over the past few years. We are burning more cash on inventory while our service levels have not improved, and one could argue might be declining."

Yusef told Bob that they were going to talk about logistics in this meeting, but he opened the discussion with something of a bombshell.

Bob crunched up the empty bottle of water and threw it at the trash can in the corner, missing it by a country mile. He didn't get up to pick up the bottle, now on the floor. He just sat and stared at it for a moment. "I thought we were going to talk about logistics. I thought this was going to be an easy discussion, Yusef. Why am I suddenly feeling uneasy?"

"We are going to talk about logistics, Boss. But I want you to understand that the problems we are having with growing inventory are most likely going to increase because of some trends we are seeing related to logistics."

"Really? That seems odd to me. Mr. Harris, do you agree? This seems like one area we could easily control," Bob questioned.

"Owens Volt Master and Volt Minnie," Yusef said before Mr. Harris could respond and offered no other explanation.

"Two of our hottest products! And two products that we often have trouble making enough of them. Don't tell me I need to worry about them?" Bob blurted.

"Boss, Volt Master, and Volt Minnie are great. So great that we are now selling them into markets we never really covered before. Last month, 12% of orders are coming from independent hardware stores. And 9% came from sporting goods stores. Two years ago, we didn't even serve these types of customers. Although the new sales have been great . . ." Before Yusef could continue, Bob cut him off.

"Hold-on! There is no 'but.' They have been great! And it's great that we have new customers. And great that we are selling into new markets. Great, great, great. No buts, Yusef."

"Boss," Yusef returned to his slow and calming voice. "Boss, sales have been great. But we increased inventory on these two products 4% faster than sales growth. We increased inventory for parts and optional components for these products 11% above sales growth. And our fulfillment rates—fulfilling orders on time—decreased 8%. We have two terrific products for which there is great demand and coming from new markets. That's good. We are building them faster than our sales growth and holding onto them longer, missing customer delivery dates and creating customer service problems because . . ." Yusef paused. He held his hand out, palm up, and gestured toward Bob prompting his boss to answer.

"Logistics?" Bob took the cue.

"You betcha!" Yusef returned to another long-running teasing of Bob's Minnesota heritage. "These new sales channels mean that we are shipping less than full pallets, adding all sorts of additional labels, and drop-shipping to hundreds of new locations. We are addressing these challenges, Boss, but it caught us off guard. We didn't have the setup to do all this without running into problems. The new labeling process alone has added an extra day to our final production steps. We didn't have enough dock space for all the smaller ship containers. Things started to get misplaced, we missed shipping windows. It has been a mess. Until we get all this sorted out, we will need to hold more inventory to meet the growing demand. I wanted to start with this story, Boss, because it highlights what we spoke of yesterday. No one made intentional decisions to build more product than we need, we just ended up here because market requirements changed and we were not prepared. When that happens, even something as seemingly straightforward as shipping can trip us up and cause a pileup of inventory."

Logistics Considerations

Mr. Harris pulled out a few sheets of paper, handing them to Bob. He and Yusef prepared for this meeting by writing down a list of some examples of logistics considerations that can affect cash flow:

- **Batch sizes:** Filling up trucks with uniform pallets can certainly save on per-unit fuel costs, but if the pallets need to be broken down and newly bundled at the point of arrival, this can add both time (lead time) and labor costs. Variations in batch size requirements need to be monitored and accounted for when planning inventory fulfillment and when considering true shipping costs.

- **Customized labeling:** Customers might require new labeling or custom packaging. This not only adds additional cost but also adds lead time and reduces flexibility. If for some reason the labeling team accidently applies too many of a customized label to packaging, this then limits what can be done with that package or might result in an expensive and time-consuming series of repackaging and relabeling steps.

- **Value-add services:** Use of technology such as radio frequency identification (RFID) is growing in popularity. Customers might seek the inclusion of RFID devices on pallets or containers to help them manage inflow and distribution. Although most customers will agree to pay a surcharge for this service, it does add additional steps to the logistics process and can take some flexibility out of the fulfillment process.

- **Incoterms:** These are widely used, standardized terms that govern situations such as transfer of ownership, insurance responsibility, required accompanying documentation and so on. Naturally issues such as ownership transfer point can have a big impact on inventory holdings, but so can mundane things like documentation. During a client plant visit years ago, I observed a very slow and cumbersome documentation process for outgoing products. Routinely, less than full vans would depart because of the backup. This caused ripple effects and drove up transportation costs considerably. (It turns out that the Wi-Fi signal was not strong enough at the dock to be reliable enough for hand-held devices, so documents were finalized across the plant floor and carried over by hand. A $49 router extender solved that problem, saving thousands of dollars in extra transportation costs.)

- **Service-level agreements:** In Chapter 2 we discussed the incentives that a buyer like Owens has in striking optimized service-level agreements with suppliers. Ideally, they want materials, goods, and services to be provided just in time and on schedule. On-time—in-full (OTIF) is a common metric for measuring this level of performance. Customers will seek service levels that are beneficial to them and hold providers accountable for OTIF. The proliferation of one-off arrangements and the extension of service levels can really grow out of control quickly if not managed carefully. Managing all these commitments can really affect logistics groups, so monitoring commitments and evaluating the business cases is important.

- **Warehouse management:** The layout of a warehouse can have significant impact on inbound and outbound flows of materials. Setting aside dedicated spaces for inspection before products are loaded on trucks (or before they are shelved in the case of inbound) helps reduce downstream quality issues. Bar code scanning is an absolute must when picking materials and putting them away. And the arrangement of inventory based on how rapidly it turns is important, grouping like products with similar demand profiles together for quicker and more reliable picking.

- **Documentation and data integration:** Sending customers regular updates on the order fulfillment process helps both parties manage OTIF expectations. Electronic messages that record order received, order processed, and order shipped date and times are common practices, and when linked to other internal processes such as billing, can save considerable administrative time and enhance the quality of the process.

Bob and Yusef spent an hour talking with Mr. Harris about these and other logistics arrangements affecting inventory and cash.

"When you asked me if I know what goes on here at Owens, I must say I was a bit put off, Yusef. I've spent most of my life building this company. But this discussion about logistics has opened my eyes. I always thought this was just about boxing things up and sending them out on trucks. But given the complex arrangements we've entered, I can see it's a great deal more than that. I also recognize that you were not saying that there is a problem with the growth of products such as Volt Master and Volt Minnie. You were trying to help me see that these new products and the new markets they serve require entirely different logistics strategies. We can't just load up uniform pallets, fill up a truck, and send all of them to a central customer location. We have many more smaller shipments that have a lot of labeling variations. We need to better anticipate changes like this so that we can adjust our fulfillment plans. It might mean we need to look at charging extra for some of these bespoke arrangements. I'm so pleased that Mr. Harris is going to help us sort through all this."

Yusef accomplished his task and as such kept quiet and offered his boss a warm smile. He learned long ago, once you've made the sale, stop selling. Bob is now understanding that inventory management is quite a bit more complex than he initially thought. To bring it all home, tomorrow he plans to take Bob to the newest Owens plant—about an hour away—so Bob can follow Caesar and see what a day in the life of a plant manager looks like.

Logistics Best Practices

Some best practices to follow:

- Take a closer look at sales logistics—the outbound fulfillment and distribution of products to your customers. Consider market changes and shifting customer requirements and ensure that you've evolved your processes to accommodate.

- You might have an opportunity to offer value-add services to your customers such as customized packaging or labeling. In some cases, you might be compelled to do this. If so, be sure you've adequately recovered the added expense. In other cases, offering premium services can give you a leg up on competition.

- In all scenarios, monitor how materials flow through this last-stage process to see if there are steps (perhaps new requirements) that are causing inventory to pile up. Don't overlook little things like the poor Wi-Fi signal. Littles things tend to add up and cause big downstream issues.

Summary

How efficiently and effectively a business receives and sends materials can have a great impact on inventory. In addition, changing customer preferences, a more global supply chain, and e-commerce can place significant new demands on logistics. There are undeniable trends toward nimbler and more responsive logistics. These can drive up costs associated with packaging and transportation, but if managed properly can also enable faster moving inventory.

5

Production

"Oh, the purple cow!" Bob lamented as he and Yusef crested the hill and saw the Owens plant in the valley. A few years earlier, a young and earnest architect suggested they paint the new factory purple. "Purple? Who paints their plant purple? Let's stick with grey," Bob argued at the time.

The young architect clearly anticipated resistance and proceeded with a soliloquy on the virtues of purple. "Rising from the field of wildflowers, this will not just be a factory, it will be a beacon. It will announce . . . no, it will shout out that this is a place of hope and optimism. Inside these purple walls great people will be doing great things. Children, passing by in yellow school buses will point excitedly at the big purple cow in the field. Purple is both regal and accessible. Purple is profound. Owens is profound. This is no ordinary factory; this is an Owens plant! This will be known as the purple cow in the valley. Great people doing great things inside!"

Silence. Bob remembers looking around the conference room. Surely this was a prank, and someone was filming him. When he finally realized that the architect was serious, he cleared his throat and thanked the young man, excusing him so the board could consider the design. In hindsight, Bob always regretted that he and the board did not wait a bit longer before they burst out laughing. Was he still in earshot? Bob, to this day, felt bad about that.

If the young architect did hear the laughter, it was he who got the last laugh. The plant was painted purple. Bob had thought the proposal so absurd he never bothered to tell his site manager to ignore the plans for the purple paint, wrongly assuming no one in their right mind would paint a 200,000 square foot building bright purple.

"Great people doing great things!" Yusef exclaimed as they approached the building. Bob just laughed. He will never admit it, but the color has grown on him. People do call it the purple cow and children passing in school busses "moo" loudly.

Bob and Yusef are met at the main plant entrance by a tall, ruggedly handsome man wearing a white hard hat. "Caesar!" Bob exclaimed. "How are you, my friend?" Caesar is a Yusef protégé. Twenty years younger, but very mature and experienced. Caesar started his career with Owens shortly after studying electrical engineering at Purdue. He is polite and deferential, but also is very confident and does not shy from sharing opinions with his leaders. Yusef wants Bob to better understand production logistics (material management), so the two will shadow Caesar for the day, getting a sense of what life is like for a plant manager.

"I'm doing great, Bob! Welcome to the purple cow!" Yusef could see Bob cringe as Caesar said that.

Inventory Material in a Plant

Let's start with some basic descriptions of inventory material in a plant. There are essentially four categories:

- **Raw inventory:** This consists of the materials that enter a plant, such as rolls of aluminum, plastic fasteners, circuit boards, and so on. These are components that will be used in the production process inside the plant. Raw materials arrive from suppliers all over the world but also might come from upstream plants within the same company. The receiving process varies greatly depending on the materials and contractual arrangements. For example, a chemical plant might receive raw materials via pipelines from petrochemical refiners, whereas Owens has a steady flow of delivery trucks arriving throughout the day.

- **Work in progress (WIP):** This is the inventory within the plant as it flows through the production process. The amount of WIP a plant has varies greatly depending on the process of production. Some products like batteries require a curing process after lead and acid are combined. Sometimes WIP can grow if there are shortages in raw materials. In the past few years, much was written about a global microchip shortage. Almost-finished automobiles piled up in lots outside factories, awaiting the installation of the critical chips. This is often referred to as trapped inventory. It can become a very costly problem for businesses, tying up precious cash at the same time as sales plunge because they can't sell half-finished goods.

- **Finished goods:** These have completed the production process but remain in the plant and on the company books awaiting final distribution. In Chapter 4 we discussed how processes such as packaging and documentation requirements can cause this inventory to build up. But there might be intentional reasons to pile up finished goods inventory. Perhaps there is a known seasonal pickup in sales so the company must prebuild in anticipation, or service-level requirements have increased, meaning that customers have a greater expectation to receive their orders on time and in full (OTIF requirements).

- **Maintenance, repair, and operations (MRO) inventory:** MRO inventory is a classification for products such as spare parts for machinery in the factory. It also includes anything required for day-to-day maintenance and operations: cleaning fluids, rubber gloves, fuel for forklifts . . . essentially, anything needed to run and maintain the plant that does not end up in the produced product.

Companies that make products need inventory. They need the raw materials, they need spare parts to fix equipment, and they need finished goods to sell. However, inventory is very expensive and can tie up a lot of precious cash. It's important to acknowledge that every dollar invested in inventory has equal value, with unequal returns, meaning, investing in inventory that sells quickly and at a high margin produces more favorable returns on the investment than inventory that sits around unused.

Caesar understands this quite well. He has been very focused on managing inventory in his plant. Often, decisions are made outside of the plant beyond his control. Knowing that, Caesar is quite disciplined with the things he can control. Owens invested heavily in software to manage materials. Often referred to as MRP, or material requirements planning, software, these programs can help calculate optimal inventory levels, taking into consideration all sorts of drivers such as lead times, batch sizes, and so on. These applications are powerful tools, but they do require continuous updates and trust.

When Caesar took over as plant manager six months ago, he started to see a pattern. The planners and material managers in the plant were creating their own stocking calculations on spreadsheets—outside of the MRP system. "What a waste," he thought. Owens spent millions of dollars on this sophisticated software application and his team was bypassing it. Not only did it seem like a waste of their systems investment also but he inherited a plant with rapidly growing inventory and deteriorating service levels. The purple cow was hoarding inventory and could not get the right finished goods out the door when expected. Caesar knew that all these one-off calculations that were being done outside the system were causing havoc.

Materials Management

The promotion to plant manager was a huge step forward in Caesar's career. He knew that was the path many of the senior leaders took at Owens. Up to this point, he spent most of his career in product development and research. There was a brief stint in marketing and customer service, but this was his first time running a manufacturing plant. With just the right amount of confidence and terror, Caesar jumped into the role. Yusef gave him the assignment to see how well he could do. The purple cow was one of the poorer performing plants, and the growing inventory levels were quite alarming. Addressing that problem was one of Caesar's first tasks. He recognized he needed help, so he sat down with Rohit in the canteen one day to get a crash course on materials management. Rohit, also new to the purple cow, was like a younger Caesar. Whip-smart and ambitious he threw himself into his new job as a materials planner. That Rohit was new also appealed to Caesar as he feared some of the old guard at the plant had grown accustomed to doing things their way and resisted change. The old guard was the first to complain that the new planning systems did not work, ignoring them in favor of spreadsheets and calculators. He needed Rohit to candidly tell him what was going on.

"Let's start by looking at five key inventory stocking categories," Rohit said as he gave Caesar a crash course after lunch. He wrote them out on a whiteboard:

- **Cycle stock:** This is the amount of inventory needed to meet current demand. For example, our forecast calls for us to produce 25 electric motors each day. We need 5 units of a certain type of metal frame for each motor. So, every day the cycle stock for that frame is 125 units. We need 125 of them to meet current projections. But do things hold constant? Are there no fluctuations in demand? No disruptions in supply and delivery? Hardly! So, we account for those scenarios by holding safety stock.

- **Safety stock:** This is our hedge against fluctuations. Because this is not a supply chain textbook, I'll spare the reader a discussion of z scores and attempt to explain in simple English. Safety stock is calculated based on historic variations in factors such as demand and lead times. On most days we needed 125 frame units, but sometimes demand surged and we needed 150 units. Or our lead time fluctuated a day or two, so we didn't always have the 125 units we need on hand. Looking at those historic fluctuations we then calculate how much we would need to have on hand based on our desired service level. A 100% service level means we never stock out. That's nearly impossible to guarantee. For example, no one foresaw all the historic disruptions the pandemic caused. Service levels are most often set between 90% and 98%. That means there would only be between a 10% and 2% chance of a stock-out for that part.

In our example, the cycle stock requirements for a certain metal frame was 125 units per day. Let's say our safety stock calculation, considering a 95% service level, calls for three more days' worth of frames. That means we would hold 500 units at any given time, and we would be 95% sure we will not stock out of those frames. Further, if you will trust me without going into the math on this, if we held 600 units instead of 500, we really don't improve the probability of a stock-out. We just spent precious cash on an extra 100 units that are not productive.

- **In-transit stock:** This is the inventory that is in transit from the supplier to the plant. Delivery times, minimum order quantities, batch sizes, and so on can affect how much we need to have in transit to meet our cycle and safety stock requirements. In Chapter 2, we discussed how saving on sourcing from low-cost, yet distant countries might not always be the best option if it means we end up with more inventory (that we own) on boats trying to get to our plants. Understanding the economic trade-offs is very important.

- **Prebuild stock:** We might elect to prebuild ahead of sea-sonal demand surges or in anticipation of plant shutdowns. Owens sells five times as many generators during the thun-derstorm season of April–July. To meet the increased demand during those four months, they add to their production in January–March prebuilding. In addition, the purple cow has a regular maintenance schedule, which requires certain equipment to be shut down for repairs. Anticipating these periods, they schedule some prebuilds to offset for the decreased production capacity.

- **Merchandise inventory:** This is the stock of finished goods required to meet sales demand. This can increase if service level commitments have been made with customers. Owens has guaranteed that Mega-Lo-Mart will receive 100 units of the popular Volt Minnie within two days of ordering, so they keep enough merchandise stock to meet that fluctuating demand requirement. They agreed to that service level because Mega-Lo-Mart is rather consistent with orders and is their largest customer for that generator. That same type of commercial arrangement might not make economic sense for other customers.

Merchandising stock should only be held for made-to-stock products. Products that are made specifically for a customer based on set orders, known as made-to-order products, should not—ideally—be held after production.

Mega-Lo-Mart also purchases custom table-top back-up power units. Owens only makes these for Mega-Lo and does so based on quarterly orders. Caesar stumbled across a corner of a warehouse at the Purple Cow filled with these power units. "Why on earth are we holding this inventory when we know the exact order Mega-Lo places each quarter?" he thought to himself. To the extent that this inventory is accumulating, it most likely indicates upstream issues, not planned-for stocking strategies.

Caesar suggested they take a quick break and grab a couple of sodas. As they approached the vending machine, Rohit could not resist the temptation to continue his tutorial. "You know, this machine is a great illustration of the difference between push versus pull inventory."

"Do you have any friends, Rohit?" Caesar said with a smile. "You really love this stuff, don't you? Please do tell me more about push versus pull."

Rohit, completely in sync with his boss's sense of humor, replied, "I used to have friends. It is so weird, though . . . everyone seems to always be busy when I call them."

"Push inventory is held according to forecasts and is most often planned for using an MRP tool. Pull inventory is much like the soda in the vending machine. This is inventory that is consumed on demand using real-time replenishment signals. A popular concept known as *kanban* was developed to improve efficiency and effectiveness succeeding in just-in-time (JIT) inventory. This means having just the right amount of material when it is needed. *Kanban* is a Japanese word meaning 'sign.' In a kanban system, visual cues or signs are used to indicate the need for replenishment."

Rohit and Caesar walked back to their conference room and resumed their discussion of the push inventory Owens has been piling up at the purple cow. "I really like Carl and Bev (the other two planners whom Rohit works with) but they don't trust the MRP to set safety stock levels. Two years ago, they ran out of switching components and the plant came to a halt. They both blamed this on over-aggressive stocking strategies the MRP calculated."

"Two years ago, Rohit? Like during the global pandemic? When everything was disrupted?" Caesar interjected.

"To be honest, I think they were looking for an excuse. They have their old ways of doing things and each maintains calculations on Excel spreadsheets. These work for the most part but are not dynamic enough to account for the rapid changes we see in some of our new product categories. Take those switches, for example. We have 21 days on hand. Even at a 99% service level, we only need 8 days. And the longest lead time we had to replenish—outside of the COVID-related spike—is 4 days, so we are carrying 9 extra days. These are expensive switches, Caesar. We've got over a million dollars in extra switches that we don't really need."

Caesar half laughed and half gasped, "A million dollars? That's almost the exact amount of capital we need to expand the Volt Minnie line to meet the increase demand. We could use that cash to dramatically increase sales, but instead it is tied up in inventory we don't need."

Rohit added to his boss's headache. "You probably know this, but the switches are highly sensitive to humidity and light. So, we had to expand the special climate-controlled storage room to continue to safely house the material. I think the last plant manager spent almost $1,000,000 doing that."

"That's why he isn't here," Caesar said to himself. The two spent the rest of the afternoon looking into issues with other stocking categories. Caesar started to ask more questions. Why, he wondered, do they have $2 million of plastic cases in transit from Vietnam? The lead time for this part is over six weeks. He knows this part well because it was a specification he worked on in product development. "Rohit, let's investigate this one as well. I fear we decided to go with a vendor in Vietnam because the unit price was lower. Let's check the math and see if we really are getting a good enough deal to offset tying up this much cash."

Caesar knew that Yusef gave him the job of plant manager to shake things up, so he and Rohit met almost every day to review inventory reports and challenge decisions.

"We've got to stop planning outside the MRP." This was the lead comment Caesar made at a meeting with his planners and material managers. He presented them data Rohit helped him compile, showing how their one-off way of planning was far more inaccurate and costly than using the parameters suggested by the system. It took some time to win over hearts and minds, but it was well worth the effort. In a matter of weeks inventory started to come down and service levels improved.

Turning the Purple Cow Around

Caesar related the previous stories to Bob and Yusef during their visit to the purple cow. He further explained that there are all sorts of demand and supply factors that can affect how much inventory is needed in the plant:

Demand-related considerations:

- Internal and external demand variations
- Forecast error rates
- Seasonal impacts
- Service level variations
- Changing customer trends
- Lags in forecast time
- Inventory outliers

Supply-related considerations:

- Batch size requirements
- Lead time requirements
- Lead time uncertainty
- Schedule variability
- Supply quality limitations
- Storage limitations
- Multiple supply sources
- Seasonal supply sources

"We set an annual budget plan about October each year," Caesar explained. "But by January it's already starting to fall apart. A couple of years back, we implemented a monthly sales

and operations planning process. We call that our S&OP process. During this monthly process we attempt to link sales forecasts with supply and production plans at the product family
level. But even this plan misses all sorts of swings and variations
and causes my planners to jump through hoops."

Caesar stood up, walked over toward the windows that overlook the factory floor, and continued. "Let me give you a few
examples." He pointed to a spot in the factory. "That's our Volt
Minnie line. Last October we added capacity to that line so we
could increase our monthly production by 15%. This was based
on the forecast and business plan our sales and marketing team
submitted. By January, sales increased by 25%. Okay. Good
problem to have. We'll somehow have to adjust to meet the
increased demand. And it wasn't a big surprise as we discussed
the trend in our monthly S&OP meetings."

He sat back down at the table. "Problem is, we change the
configuration on those machines almost every month. Each new
customer seems to want some variations. Mega-Lo-Mart wanted
the unit cost to decrease by 20% so our sourcing department
had to find less expensive suppliers. This came with new minimum order quantity requirements. Mega-Lo-Mart also wanted
a few unique features such as an enhanced grounding wire and
ground-fault circuit interrupters . . . you know, the plug with the
circuit breaker. All that is fine, but these constant changes plus
all the supply and demand considerations we discussed in the
last hour means that our S&OP process is not nearly nimble
enough. So, I introduced a weekly S&OE process. This is a sales
and operations execution process. It's far more tactical and is
focused at the stock-keeping-unit level. Now, I can anticipate
changes, even within a product family, and alter production
schedules accordingly."

Yusef looked over at Bob and smiled. He was so pleased he
picked Caesar to lead this plant. His fresh ideas and willingness to

challenge old assumptions are really paying off. Yusef had been bragging about Caesar the whole drive over to the plant. He told Bob all about the discipline he brought back to the planning process and how one change in switches freed up about a million dollars, which Caesar wisely invested in expanding the Volt Minnie line. "Caesar thinks like an investor, Bob," Yusef added. "He saw that we were making poor investments in slow-moving inventory, inventory that we did not need. And he understood the cash we tied up in those parts could be better invested to increase capacity for our hottest products. He knows how to ask questions and peel back the onion. He uses data to challenge old processes. He is nimble and adjusts plans quickly based on his new S&OE process."

"Hmm . . . maybe we have him in the wrong job, Yusef," Bob quietly said.

"Wrong job? Haven't you heard what I've said? He turned the purple cow around. He is a rock star!"

"Precisely!" Bob said more loudly. "Maybe he should have your job and head up all company operations."

Production Best Practices

Some best practices to follow:

- Pay close attention to safety stock calculations. If you have invested in MRP tools, make sure your team is using the full capability. Avoid one-off calculations and deviations from established planning processes.

- Examine in-transit stock and look for opportunities to shorten transportation windows while also decreasing

(continued)

(continued)

minimum order requirements. A steady flow of material at a constant pace is easier to work with versus erratic schedules and large quantity requirements. Implement economic trade-off processes. Be sure to account for total costs, including the cost of investing in extra inventory when considering sourcing.

- Review prebuild assumptions. When possible, build up to the point of greatest flexibility. For example, if we know the Volt Minnie as a product family will increase in demand, but we are not yet sure of the demand for customized features, build to the base-level requirements and then add or modify later as needed.

- For made-to-order inventory, there should be little to no merchandise stock on hand. If there is, challenge those assumptions and decisions that drive the need to hold that inventory.

- Implement and follow standard planning processes such as monthly S&OP and weekly S&OE processes. Document the decisions made so that you can review add adjust as needed.

- Pay close attention to maintenance schedules and be thoughtful about scheduling them, recognizing that each time a line goes down there will likely be a prebuild of inventory.

- Treat inventory dollars invested as equal to dollars invested in capital equipment or research. This brings great clarity and forces good decisions. Tying up cash in slow-moving or excess inventory is wasteful and makes for poor investments.

Summary

A plant manager can make a tremendous impact on a business. If they are willing and able to constantly challenge old ways of thinking and enforce discipline to follow established processes, precious capital can be deployed to its best use.

Before they left the purple cow, Bob and Yusef arranged to meet with the plant controller, Annette. They have heard that she has been quite innovative and has helped Caesar turn things around.

CHAPTER

6

Controller

A comedic foil is a device writers often use to create a contrast with main characters. The interplay between a staid, sober "straight man" and a hyperkinetic character can be funnier than the jokes themselves. Often the foil is overly serious and painfully literal, missing all ironic references. Playing these roles can be very demanding because it requires the actor to stay in character at all times, not giving any hint to the absurdity going on around them and squelching all impulses to break out in laughter. It's not to say these characters are removed from the comedy. Quite the opposite; they often amp up the funny factor by means of their stoic contrast.

Annette, the plant controller of the purple cow, is a comedic foil. Caesar recalls that when he first arrived at the plant he was sitting with Annette and made an off-hand comment, "Who do I have to bribe around here to get a decent cup of coffee?"

"Bribery is illegal and unethical. It violates our code of conduct," Annette responded, matter-of-factly.

Caesar thought that she was trying to be funny. Laughing a bit he said, "That's good! We are going to get along just fine." However, after the third or fourth such exchange, in which irony was lost on Annette, Caesar came to realize that she was not trying to be funny and was perhaps the most literal person he had ever met. She is very exacting in everything she does. These are not bad qualities for a financial controller to possess but her over-the-top seriousness can be quite funny. Maybe one day, at her retirement party, Annette will take off the mask and reveal that it was an act all along. If that does occur, she should win some sort of award. In the meantime, she is legendary around not just the purple cow but across the company as the most serious person to walk the face of the earth.

Yusef loves to watch Bob try to get Annette to laugh. It never works, but that doesn't deter him from trying. The topics they will discuss with her today—absorption costing, weighted average cost of capital (WACC), gross versus net working capital, and cash forecasting—reassure Yusef that his boss will strike out yet again. "Not exactly good comedy material, Boss," Yusef says as they walk toward Annette's office.

"This is my day. I can feel it! WACC? We are going to talk about WACC! I'm sure I can work with that. Today is the day we get our dear friend to crack a smile."

Absorption

Absorption costing, also referred to as *full costing*, is an accounting technique that allocates fixed cost to each unit of inventory produced. Variable cost, by contrast, just allocates the direct costs associated with producing each unit. Consider some of the products that Owens makes. The Volt Master power generator is a complicated machine in which there are thousands of components.

Those components plus labor expense, costs associated with packaging and transfers, are all allocated to each unit produced. Let's say it costs Owens $50,000 per unit for all the direct, variable inputs. But Owens also has to pay rent on the factory building and has expensive tooling machines, robotics, and assembly lines that are needed to make the generators. These are considered indirect costs.

In absorption costing, a portion of these expenses is attributed to each unit made. In our Volt Master example, let's say that the indirect costs add another $10,000 to each unit. Now, the per-unit value is $60,000 (before markup). There are two benefits to this form of accounting. First, the $10,000-per-unit cost for indirect overhead is not treated as an expense on the income statement. And second, it increases the value of inventory recorded on the balance sheet. By not hitting the income statement, net income increases (or better said—does not decrease by that amount). And gross working capital will increase. This form of cost accounting complies with generally accepted accounting principles. However, it can create some unintended consequences that negatively affect free cash flow.

By allocating indirect overhead costs to each product, an incentive arises to produce more inventory than might otherwise be needed. Let's return to our example. Let's say Owens produces 10 units of the Volt Master per month. We said that direct variable costs associated with each unit is $50,000 and the indirect overhead costs allocated to each unit is $10,000. That means our aggregate overhead costs are $100,000 per month. Now let's say that a savvy plant manager finds a way to produce twice as many units per month. The variable costs remain at $50,000 per unit, but the allocated absorption costs decrease to $5,000 per unit. Now the cost per unit before markup has seemingly reduced by 9%. Sounds good! But wait. What if demand did not change?

Demand was always 10 per month. Now we are investing a lot of cash in units we don't need given current sales.

This becomes a real issue when there is a high degree of demand volatility. There are real costs associated with setting up and altering production assets. The Volt Master is run on the same line as the Volt Minnie. It's far easier and more efficient—with a lower per-unit cost allocation—to run Volt Master in long, more continuous runs. Because of the capital equipment involved, it's time-consuming and costly to flip between Minnie and Master. But this is often how businesses end up with excess inventory.

Plant controllers like Annette can play a vital role in helping make economic trade-off decisions. Keeping on top of absorption costing and inventory build trade-offs is very important. It's even more critical when inventory has a short shelf life or when storage costs are high. If inventory has a short shelf life (food, pharmaceuticals, chemicals, etc.), producing too much not only ties up cash but also can result in costly write-downs if it expires. And storage costs can really add up. I had a client who filled every new warehouse they leased. I suggested that if we stop leasing additional space, we could bluntly get the business to come to terms with the excessive amounts of inventory they build and finally implement some remedies.

Yusef could see Bob fidgeting in his seat. He went a full 20 minutes, listening to Annette discuss absorption costing without making a joke. Now that they were going to turn to weighted average cost of capital, commonly referred to by its acronym, WACC, Bob could not hold back any longer without telling a dad joke. "Annette, I ABSORBED all that quite well! It's WACC-Y how we make some decisions around here."

"I don't think there is anything at all wacky with how decisions are made. It's really quite plain. We incentivize plant managers to find ways to run assets to full absorption. Unfortunately, this led to some decisions made without the benefit of data.

There was nothing funny at all about that," Annette said dryly. And strike one for Bob.

Weighted Average Cost of Capital

Over the course of my 30+ year career I've had the opportunity to work with a wide variety of global companies across many sectors. Each has a unique culture and DNA, but one thing I find common is a real confusion about the cost of capital. Finance executives and most senior leaders are not confused. They understand. But below the C-suite it's a mixed bag. I've wondered if that's because so much emphasis is placed on profit and loss with the balance sheet as the provenance of finance leadership. Or it's because few organizations pass along the true cost of capital to operational stakeholders. Whatever the reason, I frequently hear folks bring up the cost of short-term debt as a proxy for cost of capital. When discussing trapped cash in a business and suggesting efforts to unlock it, I've frequently been rejoined with "Yeah, but debt is so cheap right now." Or "We are swimming in cash"— that latter comment came from a relatively senior executive of a company straddled with debt.

WACC takes into account all sources (and costs) of capital such as bonds, lines of credit, commercial paper, and stock. Including the cost of equity is critically important because debt obligations and share price volatility tend to wind each other up. The more debt a company takes on, the more that risk is factored into the share price. As share prices become more volatile (have a higher beta) relative to index prices, the cost of debt also often rises. It's like a storm moving over warm waters—they start to fuel each other.

Using WACC to make investment decisions is critically important. This is often referred to as the hurdle rate. Let's say that once we consider the cost of debt plus the cost of equity, we calculate a WACC of 12%. This, then, becomes the hurdle for investment decisions. If the proposed investment is forecasted with an ROI in excess of 12%, it is worth moving forward. If it's lower than 12%, there should be serious consideration of the need for the investment. The amount of cash being allocated for the investment could be used to pay down debt and/or used to decrease the beta of equity (e.g., share repurchase). It's not that this becomes a hard-and-fast rule. There might be very good reasons to proceed with investments with projected returns below the hurdle rate, but it should be a flashing warning light. Similarly, there might be reasons prepaying debt or repurchasing stock is not advised. Perhaps the debt obligations are lower than current rates. And the market price for the stock reflects more fundamental concerns for which share buybacks will have meager positive impact. But the point about hurdle rates: it's a very useful measuring stick to evaluate investments and far more accurately reflects total cost of capital than something like the Secured Overnight Financing Rate (SOFR).

Understanding an organization's WACC is also useful in evaluating working capital performance. As mentioned, dollars invested in inventory are equal to dollars invested in everything else, but the returns on these investments differ. Even within inventory, the ROI varies based on the type of inventory. Investing in slow-moving inventory in excess of demand is much less favorable than investing in quick-moving inventory, highly in demand. Knowing that, then, the cost of implementing changes to improve inventory efficiency (i.e., investing only in things needed) should be compared against the WACC. If the cost falls below the WACC, then those actions likely make a great deal of sense.

For example, let's say that Caesar came to understand the reason his plant is holding too much inventory is due to a few factors: immature processes, training, and a lack of governance. Rohit has helped him see that he could reduce inventory by $10 million at the purple cow and can increase service levels by 400 basis points if they address these three factors. First, they need to baseline their current planning and material management processes. They then need to update those processes to reflect industry best practices. This will include updating their material requirements planning (MRP) and moving all one-off calculations into the software tool. They will need to update all their training materials, including onboarding documentation for new hires. Trainers and coaches will need to spend roughly a month with the key stakeholders so that they fully understand the new processes and know how to use and appreciate the MRP tools they have. Last, they will need to update weekly and monthly performance reports, enhance their operations review meetings, and tie performance evaluations and bonuses to adherence to the new processes and to improved inventory results.

Caesar interviewed a number of consultants and chose a firm he thought had the best experience and culture fit. It will cost Owens $800,000 to implement this program. He prepared a number of slides and graphs and sat down with Annette to get her input. Caesar knew that Annette would be a great sounding board before he went to Yusef seeking approval. Annette is impassionate and knows numbers better than anyone else. He also feels strongly about this project and did not want to look foolish and unprepared in front of his controller.

Annette listened patiently to Caesar as he explained the need for the investment and the projected benefits. She is not known to ever interrupt others. The only time Caesar can recall her interrupting him, she politely asked him to pause because she saw three fire trucks pull in front of the plant. She also never nods or gives any hint of reaction. Caesar is not even sure she blinks. He rambled a bit, as he always seems to do when talking with Annette, feeling compelled to fill any voids in a what should be a normal two-way conversation. "But, let me pause, Annette. What do you think?"

One can almost count to 10 before Annette responds to questions. "I am not in a position to evaluate the root cause of our inventory buildup nor weigh in on the solution. I am confident that you and Rohit have properly done this. But, if you are asking if we should proceed, yes we should. Our WACC is 12%. Freeing up $10 million equals a $1.2 million P&L benefit. Your program will cost $800,000. That means that even after the investment we still return $400,000 in P&L benefit. I'm sure there are hidden costs such as warehousing, handling, scrap, and so on that are tied up in our excess inventory position. That most likely makes this investment decision even better. I'm sure Carol will greatly appreciate this additional cash that she can use to help fund our dividend payment."

That was more than Annette had said all week. "That's great, Annette! I know Carol and Yusef will want your opinion. I really think this is the right thing to do. Thank you!"

"Thanking me implies that I've done you a favor. I have not. You presented me a set of facts about a proposed investment and it's my professional opinion that the investment is sound. Please don't thank me as I've not done you a favor."

"There is the Annette I know," thought Caesar.

Gross Versus Net Working Capital

Net working capital is calculated as days inventory outstanding (DIO) + days sales outstanding (DSO) – days accounts payable outstanding (DPO) Or, in other words, the amount of time it takes to convert inventory investments into sales plus how long it takes to collect money customers owe minus how long you get to pay suppliers.

Positive net working capital means that we have cash tied up in the business and negative net working capital means that we've offset the cash tied up by holding back on paying suppliers, or we get customers to pay in advance.

It's quite common for businesses to evaluate their working capital performance in *net* terms. If we know that we need to invest in a lot of inventory up-front, then we might consider commercial arrangements to offset that investment. Furniture companies often require a sizable downpayment from customers before they even start to build a sofa. There was a long-running joke in the commercial airplane business that when a customer takes delivery of a plane they get the keys to the plane plus a check for the discount they negotiated, having already remitted funds for the list price. (That joke is not quite accurate . . . but also not too far off the truth.)

In addition to focusing on net working capital, it also makes sense to look at a company's gross working capital more closely. Has inventory been increasing faster than sales? Are receivables becoming more delinquent? Those two issues could be masked at an aggregate level if they have been offset with longer payment terms. That can mask additional opportunities to generate enhanced cash flow as well as alert the business to other growing problems.

Let's say that our purchasing team has done a terrific job negotiating enhanced commercial terms. In the past we were paying suppliers in 30 days; now we are paying in 60 days. We are holding onto our cash 30 more days. But, let's also say that our past-due amount in accounts receivable (AR) has increased 20 days. Assuming no change in inventory, then our net working capital performance improved by 10 days. But, had our AR not deteriorated it could have been a 20-day improvement. And although we might congratulate ourselves on the net improvement, we lost focus on AR degradation and perhaps more serious problems such as increasing credit risk among our customer base.

Evaluating the performance of each trade working capital category (inventory, accounts receivable, and accounts payable) is a wise thing for controllers to do. In Chapter 7, we explore more closely metrics and performance indicators. But, before going into those details, I want to explain the impact of netting out working capital. Increases and decreases in sales, inflation, and strategic commodity buys can also affect net working capital and might not accurately reflect actual performance discipline.

Annette understands this. In an operations review meeting, it appeared that net working capital degraded shortly after Caesar started his inventory process improvement program. In the quarter before the initiative, the plant had on hand $150 million in inventory and $30 million in outstanding AR. They also had $40 million in outstanding AP. As they initiated new planning and forecasting processes, they started to draw down existing inventory, but, more importantly, they rapidly decreased buying new material, using up existing stock first. During that meeting, they saw a report showing inventory on hand at $145 million, AR stayed at $30 million, but AP dropped to $30 million. So it appeared that net working capital performance degraded (increased) by $5 million during that period:

- Quarter 1: $150 million inventory + $30 million AR − $40 million AP = $140 million net working capital
- Quarter 2: $145 million inventory + $30 million AR − $30 million AP = $145 million net working capital

Annette, ever calm under fire, explained to her colleagues that if they look at each component of working capital, they would see a different picture. Of course accounts payable will come down because they are buying less. They owe less to their suppliers. Inventory is coming down relative to sales, which is a very good thing, and service levels are holding constant. A net working capital snapshot is not telling the whole story. "Next Tuesday I will offer a training course in metrics," Annette offered.

"That's a great idea, Annette. I'll make sure we get the right people there. What roles should I consider?" Caesar replied.

"I'll bring bagels. You don't need to worry about rolls." The room fell silent as everyone was stunned! Did she really just tell a joke? Has this been an act all along? No one knew what to say next. Annette broke the silence with, "I'm sorry for being so silly. I know you meant job roles. I will send a list to you tomorrow."

Caesar could not wait to call Yusef and tell him!

Cash Forecasting

Canned green beans and canned tuna. That was my diet several days each month the year after I graduated college; I was on my own and managing my budget. I got paid on the 1st and 15th of each month. So, on the 13th, 14th, 30th and 31st of most months I had run out of cash and had to economize. So I resorted to eating like a house cat—tuna out of a can. I thought adding canned green beans would make it healthier or perhaps a bit more responsible—I'm not really sure. That experience taught me a valuable lesson about managing cash flow. It also taught me to appreciate hot meals when I could get them!

Forecasting cash is critically important and yet most organizations I speak with admit they don't do a great job of it. I was able to adjust my spending and could tolerate eating canned tuna because I knew that I was soon to be paid. There would be an influx of cash. I also was very careful about managing my expenses.

I knew rent was due on the 1st. My utility payments were due a week later and I set my car payment up on the 16th. I was able to balance my debt obligations to align with my known income.

But what if my employer did not pay me on the 1st and 15th? What if I knew I would get the same amount of money but was never sure which day of the month? Oh, and what if my landlord randomly stopped in each month asking for rent? I would have the same amount of income and the same debt obligations, but I lost control of receipts and disbursements. If that happened, I'd have to hold back and keep more cash on hand because I would not know when I'd get more or know when I would need to pay my bills.

On a much bigger scale, the same sort of dynamic plays out at most companies. Not the tuna and beans part, but the consideration of holding enough cash to meet obligations. If an organization struggles to accurately forecast receipts and disbursements, then they will decrease their flexibility to deploy the cash to its most productive sources. It might require a greater dependence on debt facilities such as commercial paper. And variances in reported cash positions can really spook investors. Even positive swings, such as ending up with more cash than projected point to potential process failures.

Keeping it simple, there are two methods of cash forecasting: direct and indirect. Direct forecasting is a bottom-up approach that is based on actual cash flow data, rolled up from operating units in the business. Indirect forecasting relies on models to project likely outcomes. In reality, most organizations use a mix of both methods. If we are projecting an outcome quarters or months out, some form of indirect or model/scenario-based forecast will be used. As we get closer in, then a sweep of actual results will be used. The tricky part is reconciling the gap between model-based forecasts and actual results.

Data and systems complexity can make this process opaque. Yet, it is important to examine forecasting processes and work toward improved accuracy.

The goal behind improving the generation of operating cash flow is to be able to use the extra cash for more productive purposes with higher rates of return. In order to do that, organizations need to forecast when they will receive cash and when they need to disburse cash to meet payment obligations. Think back to my example of my first year out of college. I ran a very efficient personal cash management program because I had to. Fortunately, I had easy-to-predict receipt and disbursement cycles so that I didn't need to hold back any additional cash in my checking account than I really needed. Thank goodness I was able to limit my tuna-and-bean days to roughly four days per month!

Best Practices for Controllers

Some best practices to follow:

- Adopt a practice of reviewing absorption costing at the plant or business unit level and compare against inventory levels. Are we doing well on absorption metrics at the cost of running up inventory?

- Conduct operations reviews to better understand how and why fixed costs have been allocated.

- Be disciplined about calculating your true WACC and use that calculation to evaluate investment decisions.

- Avoid making decisions relating to cash (preservation/deployment) based on current cost of debt such as the

(continued)

(continued)

Secured Overnight Financing Rate (SOFR). During periods when the SOFR rate is low, a "free money" attitude, which does not consider cost of equity, can creep in.

- When looking at net working capital, be careful to not let that distort the art of the possible for optimal working capital performance. Strong performance in one category of working capital can hide poor performance in another area.

- Similar to the net versus gross working capital performance, be careful when aggregating performance across a business with different operating units. At the aggregate level, a high-performing business unit might mask a poor-performing unit. It's important to evaluate opportunity at the operating unit level.

- Pay close attention to the accuracy of your cash forecasting process. Variability or inaccuracy in forecasting can negate much of the goodwill created through improved operating cash processes. The goal is to deploy cash to its most productive uses.

Summary

In summary, a good controller will be on top of accounting and financial reporting. A great controller will use that insight and data to help the business make more informed decisions.

"She said she would bring the bagels!" Caesar emphasized the punchline of Annette's joke to Bob and Yusef. The three laughed and also discussed the theory that her straight-as-an-arrow, deadpan way of communicating must really be an act after all. Whether an act or not, it endeared them to her all the more.

Yusef suggested they include Annette in the upcoming session to review metrics and reporting. "She clearly is doing an outstanding job, providing her plant with expert advice and guidance. And . . . maybe, just maybe, Boss, you can get her to smile after all!"

7

Metrics

What's measured, improves.

—Peter Drucker

What do think of when contemplating metrics? When you saw that there is a chapter on the subject, did you skip ahead to this page with great anticipation? It's hard to know if we've made progress or if we are somehow falling behind unless we capture measurements. And, oh, do we love to measure things! Most organizations measure everything in sight whether the information is useful or not. This leads to complacency and lack of understanding for what is really going on.

We live in a DRIP world: data rich, information poor (coined by Tom Peters and Robert Waterman in their seminal book *In Search of Excellence*). We measure a lot of things but fail to use all that data to make effective decisions or change processes.

Bob has long feared that Owens struggles with this. It's a company filled with engineers, and they really love to measure stuff. So, it was a bit counterintuitive that Bob decided to task Arthur with a review of Owens's metrics. Arthur is the chief engineer and although he does not actually wear a pocket protector, he certainly does live up to many stereotypes of engineers. Then again, he does defy some of the stereotypes because he is known to play part-time in a rock band.

"Art, rumor has it that you are in a band. Is that true?" Bob is the only one who calls Arthur Art. Or maybe the only one who gets away with it.

Arthur chuckled. "Yeah, it's a few guys from my neighborhood. We drive our families nuts, practicing in our basements and garages."

"Does the band have a name?"

"We are called Algainti. We play mostly heavy metal."

Bob responded, "Al-whaty?"

"Algainti," Arthur said with a mischievous tone. He went on to explain that the name of the band is a mash-up of elements from the periodic table: Al, Ga, In, Ti . . . all are part of a group of elements frequently referred to as poor metals. Their band that plays mostly heavy metal rock is named after a group of poor metals. "Fitting, huh?"

Bob laughed. Indeed, it is fitting. Only Arthur, he thought to himself, would come up with a name like this. He is such a classic nerd that it's kind of cool. Arthur comes across as geek chic. And, who better to look at metrics being used at Owens and advise the leadership team on possible changes? Because Bob is really focused on cash, he asked Arthur to start with a review of metrics, key performance indicators (KPIs), and measurements that focus on Owens's cash position. "Please report back to the leadership team about your thoughts on the metrics we should be using to foster a cash culture," Bob instructed.

As Bob was making the rounds, talking with people such as Jeremy, Carol, Yusef, Caesar, and Annette, one thing became very clear to him. To achieve desired outcomes, the organization must set targets and deploy metrics that motivate and guide individuals. However, as Owens has grown and become more complex, they kept adding all sorts of KPIs and ways of measuring things. This not only consumes time and resources but also it reduces the impact of the important things that management should be looking at. It will be hard for Bob to turn things around if he can't hold people accountable for improved performance, and to do that, he needs to be sure the organization is focused on the right set of metrics.

Arthur was, however, a bit reluctant to take on the assignment when Bob first approached him. "I'm not a finance guy, Bob. If you are looking for the best metrics to promote cash, don't you want Carol or someone from finance leading the cause? I don't know anything about treasury or cash."

"Precisely! Art, I want you to do this because I want the metrics to make sense to you. And if they make sense to you, they will make sense to others outside of finance. To create a cash culture, we need everyone in the business to recognize the impact they have. Carol and I can't make every decision. We need people tasked in a way that gets them rowing in the same direction." Bob was thinking back to the funny boat model that Yusef has—with oars going in every direction.

As we examine common cash-related metrics, let's first consider what we are trying to achieve. Do we need indicators alone or do we need data that will guide decisions? To explain this last question, think of the difference between the fuel gauge on your car and the speedometer. The fuel gauge is just telling you how much gas you have burned and how much you have left. Other than pulling over or possibly turning off the AC, this gauge doesn't really influence your current actions. The speedometer, however, helps you stay within proscribed limits. On my car I was able to program an alarm to go off when I exceed a certain limit. I confess that I set that alarm to go off at a speed quite far above any normal highway speed limit. That's the other thing about metrics—just because they are in place, does not ensure compliance. We'll pick up that concept a bit later.

For publicly traded companies there are two required types of cash-related reports:

- **Balance sheet:** Measures a company's assets, liabilities, and shareholder equity at a certain point of time
- **Cash flow statement:** During a specific period, records the cash a business receives and spends

It's important to note the difference between balance sheet health and cash flow. A company can have a positive cash flow during a period, receiving more cash than it consumes, but its balance sheet might be constrained if it is also highly in debt. Conversely, a company sitting on a pile of cash can endure periods of a negative cash flow and remain highly liquid. When we talk more about resiliency this concept will be revisited.

Types of Metrics

There are many additional cash metrics that management, analysts, and investors often use to assess the health of the business. The following are some of the common metrics.

Days Inventory Outstanding (DIO)

This measures the average number of days inventory is held before it is sold. This is like golf . . . lower numbers are better. Calculate this by taking the value of inventory on hand and divide by cost of goods sold (COGS), then multiply by 365. This yields the average number of days it takes to convert inventory into cash.

Example: There is $500,000 of inventory on hand and the COGS for the period is $2,000,000.

($500,000/$2,000,000) × 365 = 91 days inventory on hand

COGS measures the direct costs that are inputs into goods. Cost of sales also includes the indirect costs associated with selling the product. Generally speaking, COGS is the preferred denominator for most businesses that make and sell products because it will more closely show the direct costs tied up in inventory. Services businesses and retailers might prefer using cost of sales because the cost of the good is more of a pass-through and the real measured cost of the inventory on hand is the indirect overhead associated with sales.

Days Payable Outstanding (DPO)

Measures the average number of days it takes to pay suppliers. Unlike golf, the higher the number tends to be better. Ideally, we'd like to hold onto cash as long as possible before paying vendors, but it is true that there are very real limits on acceptable behavior. In some cases, there are government regulations that stipulate payment terms for certain commodities or in certain jurisdictions. There is also a cobweb of contracting requirements when working with the federal government. But, suffice to say, we tend to look for longer AP days to offset the days of inventory on hand and the days it takes us to get paid. DPO is calculated by taking the amount of trade payables owed divided by COGS (or sales) and then multiplied by 365.

Example: The amount of payables currently owed is $300,000 and COGS is $2,000,000

($300,000/$2,000,000) × 365 = 54 days payable outstanding

Days Sales Outstanding (DSO)

This measures the average number of days it takes to collect money from customers during a period. Back to golf: a fewer number of days is better. We want to get paid as quickly as possible. To calculate, take the amount of AR open, then divide that by the sales during that period, and last multiply the result by the days in the period. Let's stick with a year as we did previously.

Example: The amount of open AR is $915,000 and annual sales is $4,500,000.

($915,000/$4,500,000) × 365 = 74 days sales outstanding

Cash Conversion Cycle

This measures the time it takes a business to convert to cash what it spends on inventory. We are still on the golf course—the lower the number means we convert to cash more quickly. The formula is: CCC = DIO + DSO − DPO

Example: Using the DIO, DPO, and DSO calculations we used previously, it takes 111 days to convert the input costs into cash.

91 (DIO) + 74 (DSO) − 54 (DPO) = 111 (CCC)

CCC will vary by the type of business. Some firms require longer production processes and therefore will tie up cash longer. Others can convert more quickly. This metric is useful to compare similar businesses against each other. We will talk about benchmarking a bit later, and I'll offer a disclaimer that CCC comparisons are directionally correct, but rarely do competing businesses have the exact same makeup of products and markets. These differences can affect CCC rates. And yet, CCC comparisons are directionally accurate.

Looking at CCC fluctuations for a specific business over time can also be helpful in evaluating the health of a firm. If CCC is creeping up as the business grows, it might be because it is producing more complex products that require more production time. Yet, it might really reflect creeping complexity in collections, enabling AR balances to grow. Either way, just like a golf score or our body weight, reductions tend to be much better than increases.

Current Ratio and Quick Ratio

Both of these ratios evaluate liquidity and the ability of a business to pay off debt. Quick ratio tends to be more conservative and considers only those things that can convert to cash quickly, such as in 90 days. Current ratio expands the consideration further to include inventory and allows for a longer period of conversion such as one year.

- **Quick ratio:** (AR, marketable securities, and so on that can be sold within 90 days)/(current liabilities such as AP, short-term debt and accrued expenses)
- **Current ratio:** (current assets such as AR, marketable securities, inventory that can be sold with a year)/(current liabilities)

Both ratios are useful to inform creditors and investors of the firm's ability to meet liability obligations. Quick ratio considers a shorter term to meet obligations, and it is more conservative it might be overly so in some cases because it does not take into consideration real value that exists in inventory that could be sold off. Conversely, current ratio might be too optimistic because it does not consider inventory obsolescence or the cost of discounting if the firm must quickly sell those assets.

Working Capital Turnover Ratio

This metric shows how efficient a company is at converting working capital into sales. Although a higher ratio is most often better, a ratio that is growing too quickly over time can indicate the need for additional capital to support sales growth. The calculation for this metric is as follows:

Net sales/Working capital

Net sales are the firm's gross sales over the course of the year minus discounts, rebates, returns, and so on. For the calculation of working capital, we use current assets − current liabilities. In other words, we count the cash on hand + marketable securities (that can be liquidated in a year) + inventory + accounts receivable, and then we subtract cash outlays in the year, or current liabilities. These are accounts payable (what we owe) and short-term debt that is due in the year.

Example: Let's say Blue Bird industries had $5,000,000 in net sales and $8,000,000 working capital.

Net sales of $5,000,000 = $5,750,000 (gross) − $750,000 (rebates and sales returns)

Working capital of $8,000,000 = $10,000,000 (current assets) − $2,000,000 (current liabilities)

$5,000,000 / $8,000,000 = Working capital turnover ratio of 63%

Now, compare that to Snowy Owl Inc., which had sales of $3,000,000 and $3,100,000 of working capital. Their turnover ratio is 97%.

Snowy Owl converts a higher percentage of its working capital into sales than does Blue Bird. We can conclude that Snowy Owl is more efficient. But let's say that over the next couple of quarters, Snowy Owl's conversion ratio starts growing quickly and rises to 136%. This is now worth examining. It might mean that Snowy Owl has become really great at converting working capital into sales, but it might also indicate something of a limitation on sales growth. Snowy Owl may need to invest in more capital to sustain higher rates of sales growth.

It's important to reinforce that the metrics we are discussing, including working capital turnover, are just indicators and they don't provide exact answers about the health of companies. I'm reminded of President Harry Truman's frustration with economists who would describe a scenario with near certainty and then turn around saying, "but on the other hand . . ." He quipped that he needed a one-armed economist. Metrics behave similarly; they need to be looked at over periods of time, evaluating swings in performance and evaluated against peers or similar businesses.

Burn Rate

This is a quick measure of the number of months before an entity runs out of cash at the current rate of consumption. Looking at burn rates is very important at evaluating start-up companies or those in financial distress. Arthur has firsthand experience with this. He has always been interested in music; hence, Algainti, the band he formed.

A few years back he met two young musicians, Dom and Elaine, who started a business staging and promoting rock concerts. The concerts featured mostly local (and aging) rockers like Arthur. They had successfully pulled off three concerts in nearby college towns and were seeking investors for a more ambitious destination concert. Their vision was to create a three-day event, featuring 40 bands at a farm about 50 miles away.

Arthur was intrigued. Dom told him they needed another $20,000 to pull it off, showing him dreamy profit figures. A third of the tickets would be presold so they would have cash up front. They would make half of their money selling parking spots as well as t-shirts and souvenirs. The bands would get a cut of just the ticket sales, and they would be paid after the event. The farmer agreed to a fixed $30,000 payment for the use of his property: the first $15,000 payment was due at the signing of the contract, which Dom and Elaine paid. Smartly, they formed a limited liability company (LLC) with $30,000 cash from past ventures. Arthur's $20,000 infusion would give him a 25% stake in the business. Nikki, Arthur's wife, was not thrilled with the idea, but gave him her blessing to pursue his dream of being the next big music mogul . . . of the county. The new business was called Wood Shock.

Wood Shock had $35,000 cash on hand after the $15,000 they paid to Farmer Brown. Yes, his name was really Farmer Brown. Even worse it was Farmer Charles Brown. What could go wrong? It turns out that Dom and Elaine had not really thought through this business idea, nor had they done much homework. For events with more than 200 people, the county requires a permit. For an event of a few thousand, as they thought Wood Shock could draw, they would also need to hire off-duty sheriff's deputies, have on-site medics and an ambulance, plus portable toilets, generators, tanks of drinking water, cooling tents, fencing, catering for the bands . . . it went on and on. It took all of Nikki's control to not tell Arthur she told him so!

With six months to go before the event, ticket sales were trickling in at the rate of about $10,000 per month. However, expenses were now accumulating at a rate of about $18,000 per month. Even though Arthur claims to not be a financial expert, he did understand basic math.

Arthur sat down with Dom and Elaine and explained burn rate to them. With $35,000 on hand and a steady flow of $10,000 in cash coming in from ticket sales, the $18,000 out the door each month in expenses did not initially alarm Dom and Elaine.

However, Arthur explained that unless cash receipts increase or expenses decrease, they will run out of cash in five months:

Five months to concert: $35,000 + $10,000 − $18,000 = $27,000

Four months to concert: $27,000 + $10,000 − $18,000 = $19,000

Three months to concert: $19,000 + $10,000 − $18,000 = $11,000

Two months to concert: $11,000 + $10,000 − $18,000 = $3,000

One month to concert: $3,000 + $10,000 − $18,000 = ($5,000)

Even though all indications point to a surge of same-day ticket sales as well as sales of t-shirts, souvenirs, parking fees and so on, Wood Shock will need more capital to survive. On paper, it could be a profitable venture, but the timing of cash coming in and going out was the problem. It had a burn rate that was not sustainable.

Somehow convincing Nikki, Arthur chucked another $15,000 into the venture. Dom and Elaine gave up ownership control, so the engineer-rocker now was concert producer as well. Wood Shock did make a small profit and it taught the young entrepreneurs an important lesson about free cash flow and how even profitable businesses can go belly up if cash burn exceeds liquidity on hand.

Price to Cash Flow Ratio (P/CF)

If you've made it this far in reading this book, I hope the drum-beat message of the importance of cash is pounding away in your ears. Look at the cover again. Cash is king. Profitable businesses can go out of business without adequate cash. Good ideas can't get launched, new products can't be developed, markets cannot be expanded without cash. Cash is also highly dependent on timing. There needs to be a positive balance between inflow and outflow. It should not be surprising, therefore, that investors look at price to cash flow ratios when considering investments. The ratio considers share price in relationship to cash generation, or how much an investor is willing to pay for dollars of cash generated. The higher the ratio, the more they are willing to pay.

This ratio makes sense when looking at sectors or types of businesses. Mature, slower-growth businesses tend to have lower ratios than high-growth newer companies. Investors are essentially signaling they are willing to take more of a risk in terms of cash coverage if the business is perhaps a fast-growth tech company. But, comparing P/CF among similar companies, an investor can see if valuation of the share price is signaling a concern about the firm's cash position. Some would say this ratio is a more accurate assessment of the health of a company than the frequently used price to earnings (P/E) ratio. As we discussed, earnings can be manipulated, making P/E ratios look more favorable than they ought to be. It's really hard to manipulate P/CF ratios . . . you either have the cash or you don't. Here is how P/CF is calculated:

Share price/(Trailing cash flow/Shares outstanding) = P/CF ratio

Trailing cash flow is the average over a period of time, typically the previous 12 months. This is useful to avoid spikes up or down that might skew results. Let's say there are 100,000 shares of company ABC; the share price is $20 and the trailing cash flow average is $180,000. Then the P/CF ratio is 11:

$20/($180,000/$100,000) = $11

This tells us that investors are willing to pay $11 for every $1 of cash generated over the course of a 12-month period. If company DEF, a rival of ABC, has a P/CF ratio of $7, then investors are not willing to pay as much for DEF to generate cash as they are for ABC. It could be because ABC has some new patent or a valuable contract, but it also could be that investors are leerier of DEF's ability to generate cash or its debt exposure. P/CF ratio provides an indicator, not a comprehensive answer. But, it's a good and reliable indicator based on what investors value.

Aligning on the Metrics

Arthur needed to get up and walk around the office. He had spent all morning looking into various metrics that Owens uses for external reporting purposes, and before he turned to consider those used inside the company, he needed to take a break.

There is a ping-pong table in the canteen—he walked over and found his newest victim. Keeping with his geek-chic personality, Arthur is quite accomplished at table tennis. Everyone at Owens calls the game *ping-pong*; he insists on referring to it as table tennis. Something of a hustler, he doesn't let on to his advanced skills until after he lures in his opponents. But, by this time, he has played and beaten just about everyone at Owens. Yusef had to stop him, when Arthur tried to play a delivery boy for money. The stakes were only $10, but Yusef knew that the kid had no chance.

Ideally, metrics that are used by leadership are fed upward by operational indicators. And, equally important, operators of the business need to have tools and metrics available to them that support their daily activities, showing them impacts of their actions. Unfortunately, it's more often the case that the metrics used at the top of the house are not aligned with those used within operations. This might be due to data integration problems— multiple sources of data that don't "talk to each other." It also is likely that no one has ever embarked on a comprehensive review of what is being captured and how it is being used.

After he handily beat Alice from HR and Toby, one of the cooks in the canteen, Arthur set aside his personal ping-pong paddle and went back to the conference room where he and a couple of junior engineers from his department would now look at internal, operational metrics. Yes, Arthur has his own ping-pong paddle . . . complete with leather case and emblazoned with a big yellow Michigan M.

Metrics Terminology

In this section, we will look at some operational metrics and common terms associated with trade working capital performance. These are terms and tactical metrics that measure the performance of inventory, accounts receivable, and accounts payable.

Inventory Metrics and Terminology

These are terms you need to know related to inventory metrics:

- **Days inventory outstanding (DIO):** We examined this previously. It measures the amount of inventory on hand as expressed by days based on current levels of consumption (or sales) of that inventory.

- **Inventory turns:** This measures the number of times inventory is sold or used during a given period of time.

- **Inventory stock to sales ratio:** This measures the amount of inventory being held relative to sales. A low ratio is generally a good thing, but it can signal potential for stock-outs. And conversely a high ratio indicates there will not be lost sales due to a shortage of inventory, but it also can signal too much cash investment is tied up as well as growing costs associated with inventory storage and management.

- **Slow-moving or obsolete inventory (SLOBS):** This is a common term used to identify inventory that turns slowly or that has a high stock to sales ratio. Often, this inventory becomes obsolete if it far exceeds demand.

- **Gross margin return on investment (GMROI):** People commonly refer to this as **Jim Roy.** This measures the profitability of inventory. Mostly used in a retail environment, it shows how much profit is derived from each dollar of cash invested in bought inventory.

- **Cost per unit:** This considers both fixed costs and variable costs associated with making a unit of inventory. This tends to decrease as volume increases because the fixed costs are spread out over a larger quantity.

- **Inventory accuracy:** There is frequently a difference between physical inventory on hand and inventory accounted for in the books. There might be a number of factors that affect accuracy, such as poor warehouse management processes, incorrect labeling, or shrink (see later in this list).

- **Cycle count:** This refers to a process of auditing inventory accuracy. Using sample batches, inventory is counted on a continuous basis and then statistical models project overall accuracy. An actual physical count of inventory can be quite disruptive, often stopping all production. Cycle count provides for an effective proxy.

- **Shrink:** Inventory shrink refers to the difference between recorded inventory and actual inventory. Causes of shrink often include damage, lost items, theft, and clerical errors.

- **Shrink as percent of sales:** This is a common metric used in the retail sector. It can help call out performance among stores or divisions in managing physical inventory. Rising levels of shrink to sales might indicate poor handling and storage processes or an increasing problem with theft.

- **Forecast accuracy**: Tricky things are forecasts. As discussed in Chapter 5 we rely on forecasts to drive business decisions. But, even with all sorts of data points, a forecast is ultimately a bet on an outcome. We think there will be increased demand for a new product, so we buy materials and build those products chasing that perceived demand. When we get it right, we buy only what we need and build to fulfill orders on time. Measuring forecast accuracy is important as we continually look to identify opportunities to improve the process.

- **Forecast bias:** Similar to measuring forecast accuracy, measuring bias is key because it looks at errors over time and indicates whether we under- or over-forecasted demand. We refer to this as bias because frequently we tip the scales one way or the other based on gut instinct, past occurrences, and so on. A positive bias means that we under-forecasted demand and likely missed sales due to lack of inventory. A negative bias is the opposite and we were too optimistic about demand and now have too much inventory.

  Although both negative and positive biases have consequences, most organizations tend to err on the side of a negative bias. If we stock out of something and miss a sale, a lot of people know about it. Customers are disappointed and complain. Sales teams are frustrated because they are losing revenue on which they earn commissions, and marketing departments fret over giving up market share to competitors. A few of these misses and folklore starts to set in: people tend to mistrust the processes and then overcompensate. We are biased to overstating the potential for demand and we end up with too much inventory. There are trade-offs between making positive- and negative-biased forecasts. It's just that more attention gets paid to positive biases than negative. Both need to be examined as negative biases tie up precious cash.

- **On-time—in-full (OTIF) percentage:** Measures a firm's ability to meet delivery requirements according to the agreed-on schedule (on time) and the contracted amount (in full). Delivering orders late can cause all sorts of downstream problems. If we are the recipient of material that is perennially late, we might have to add excess inventory to buffer against the missed plans. This costs money. Conversely, it's also not helpful if our supplier sends inventory ahead of schedule. This can trigger premature transfer of ownership— again, we take on more inventory than we need at that point in time, and it can really gum up the receiving process, particularly if our facility lacks the space to store excess materials. Recall that Jeremy had to deal with a bunch of semi-trailers sitting outside the docks, in the parking lot, because suppliers were sending materials ahead of the planned dates.

- **Supplier quality metrics:** Once Jeremy introduced supplier score cards and started to keep metrics, Owens was able to work with their suppliers to improve OTIF rates. Keeping track of metrics such as OTIF as well as defect or damage rates, labeling or packaging adherence, documentation accuracy, and so on is a key part of managing inbound materials. We strive to have just what we need at the right time, in the right place, and to the right specifications. It's also valuable to hold that mirror up to ourselves as we ship products to our customers. Understanding the quality of fulfillment from our suppliers and quality to our customers has a big impact on how much we have to invest in inventory.

Accounts Payable Metrics and Terminology

These are terms you need to know related to accounts payable metrics:

- **Days payable outstanding (DPO):** Previously in this chapter we looked at how this is calculated. DPO measures the average time a company takes to pay its vendors. The higher the number tends to be better, because we can hold onto cash longer.

- **Accounts payable balance:** This is the total amount we owe vendors. This does not include payroll, nor does it include debt.

- **Weighted average terms for accounts payable (WAT/AP):** This measures the average commercial terms a company has with its vendors. Let's say the Snowy Owl Inc. has WAT/AP of 45 days. That means that, on average, Snowy Owl Inc. has negotiated the right to pay suppliers in 45 days.

- **Weighted average days to pay (WADTP):** This measures the average time it takes a firm to pay its suppliers. We said Snowy Owl Inc. had WAT of 45 days, but because of a backlog in its AP department and process issues, their WADTP is actually 55 days. So, on average they pay 10 days late . . . 10 days longer than the terms they negotiated. Blue Bird Co. has the opposite issue. Someone decided to start paying as invoices arrived, and they prepaid ahead of holidays and weekends. Their WAT are also 45 days but their WADTP is at 30 days. Blue Bird is paying suppliers 15 days too fast.

- **Weighted average purchase order term (WAPOT):** Typically, payment terms are negotiated with suppliers and memorialized in contracts called master services agreements (MSAs). And, as we discussed in Chapter 2, purchase orders (POs) specify quantity, price, delivery dates, and so on. Ideally the payment terms on a PO should match the payment terms in the MSA. But not always. It's important to perform periodic reviews to ensure we capture the most favorable of the two terms if they differ.

- **Terms adherence:** The difference between WAT and WADTP can present either a positive or negative situation for a company. But even when it favors them positively, too big a gap can cause problems down the road. Suppliers get frustrated when payments are erratic, and they can't forecast their cash. Ideally, we are up-front with commercial terms, and we pay accordingly.

- **Payment trigger:** When does the payment clock start? What is the triggering event? Often the default trigger is the date on the invoice. This is problematic because the vendor might be quite late in sending the invoice, or maybe they sent it to the wrong location, and it took days of internal routing. Not to mention how easy it is to manipulate the invoice date. If Snowy Owl Inc. has 45-day terms and the date on the invoice is June 1st, then it is due on July 15th. But what if the vendor was slow in sending and Snowy Owl received the invoice June 20th? That means they now only have 25 days left to pay the invoice according to terms. This means treasury has fewer days to move funds around and likely causes all sorts of issues with their overall cash forecasting. Invoice receipt date is a far better trigger. When the company receives the invoice, the clock starts. Why should Snowy Owl suffer because the vendor had poor billing processes? If it arrived on June 20, then they should have until August 4th to pay.

- **Payment frequency:** This refers to how often during the month a firm makes payments. A very common practice is to pool invoices and pay them twice per month and to do so in arrears. (In arrears means paying after the date, not before.) Let's say Snowy Owl has decided they will now pay in arrears on the 1st and 15th of every month. That means the 45-day clock must end on or before those dates. If their supplier manages to get the invoice in, so that Snowy Owl receives it on June 1st, then they can expect to be paid July 15th. However, if they send it in on June 5th, then 45 days later is July 20th. The next payment run will be August 1st and that is when the vendor will be paid.

Some find this controversial. I've had heated debates with some buyers who find this troublesome. There will be certain categories of spend such as tax, utility, and rent payments in which a grace period such as this won't work. But I can say that many companies have adopted this practice and it has become the norm. Although it does, no doubt, add to the weighted average days to pay, it is relatively easy for a supplier to pinpoint the actual payment date and forecast accordingly. Suppliers want their money as quickly as possible, as we do from our customers. But, predictability and accurate forecasts are also quite important.

Perhaps just as common, and I would argue far more controversial, is the notion of withholding payments at the end of a reporting period to give the appearance of a higher accounts payable balance. Example: Snowy Owl decides to hold back $8 million of payments from June 10th through the rest of the month and then pay those in July. At the close of the second quarter, their AP balance looks to be $8 million higher. It's a bit of window dressing and it also drives suppliers nuts. They have no way of knowing this is happening until after the fact and they end up missing their quarterly projections because their AR balance went up. A supplier— I believe—would rather accept a new payment frequency policy that is accurate compared to an arbitrary withholding they can't predict.

Accounts Receivable Metrics and Terminology

These are terms you need to know related to accounts receivable metrics:

- **Days sales outstanding (DSO):** Again, this formula and metric was described. But as refresher, DSO measures the number of days on average to collect money that customers owe.

- **Weighted average terms for accounts receivable (WAT/ AR):** This measures the average commercial terms a company has with its customers. If Snowy Owl Inc. has WAT/ AR of 35 days, it means that, on average, customers have negotiated to pay Snowy Owl in 35 days.

- **Weighted average days to collect (WADTC):** This measures the average time it takes customers to pay. In Chapter 1 Carol signaled the alarm with Bob that even though Owens had on average 35 day terms, it was taking the company 65 days on average to collect payment. She told Bob that Owens had become a bank because it was floating their customers an extra 30 days beyond contractual obligations.

- **Best possible DSO (BPDSO):** This is the best-case scenario if everyone paid exactly on time to the terms negotiated. The delta between BPDSO and DSO reflects failures. The gap might be because billing is slow and cumbersome and therefore customers receive invoices late. Smart customers start the payment trigger when the invoice arrives. Or it could be because documentation was inaccurate such as PO references. Perhaps there was a quality issue with the products sent and the customer doesn't want to pay the full amount. Or, it might even be due to sloppy credit review processes, when we agreed to sell to deadbeat customers with dodgy credit histories. Either way, the delta represents money we should have, but don't, and now we must spend more money and energy trying to chase it down and claw it back.

In certain sectors there are a few powerful customers who can dictate commercial terms. For example, the grocery sector in the US is dominated by a handful of retailers. To sell into this sector means that one mostly likely does not have much bargaining power with regard to commercial sales terms. And yet, because these retailers are highly dependable, any gap between BPDSO and DSO is most likely an internal point of failure within the control of the supplier.

- **AR balance:** This is the cumulative amount customers owe at a given point in time.

- **Past due percentage:** This measures the percentage of open accounts receivable that is past the due dates. Ideally this would be calculated for every invoice based on actual due dates, but commonly this is the amount still owed after the end of the month. So, something that was due on the 10th of the previous month and not paid is lumped in with something due on the 20th of that month. In addition, some don't really start to look at this until the past due is over 30 days or even over 60 days. Using the previous example, if the bill was due on the 10th and we wait until the next month to add it to our past due bucket, it might not show up on reports until another month later. By that point it's a full 50 days late.

- **Bad debt provision:** This is an accounting reserve set aside for the write-down of bad debts. It's a cruel fact that even with best processes in place, some bills will not be paid. These must be written off. To account for that, an estimate is made based on historic performance, and this is recorded as a negative asset on the balance sheet.

- **Cycle time to identify disputes:** This and resolution time (described next) is a very important metric that too often gets overlooked. In our grocery retailer example, we said that those retailers pay consistently (no games) as long as the invoice, shipment, documentation, and so on is accurate. If there is a problem and the retailer is holding back payment, this is called a dispute. How quickly a firm identifies these disputes is very important. Perhaps the shipping department sent six pallets instead of the seven called for in the order. Ideally, this would set off an alert that the customer is likely not going to pay until the missing pallet arrives. Measuring this cycle time along with the type of dispute will help identify corrective actions that can be taken and will, over time, close the gap between BPDSO and DSO.

- **Cycle time to resolve disputes:** This is a cousin to the identification metric. This one measures how long it takes to resolve the dispute once identified. For this metric to be truly useful, there needs to be a very easy to understand categorization of disputes. In the short shipment example, ideally the category for that would be something straightforward such as "incomplete shipment." If, however, the categories are vague and someone selects "problem with order," then it will be very hard to determine if the amount of time resolving this type of dispute is getting better or worse over time.

- **Closed loop dispute resolution:** This is the holy grail. Not only do we want to quickly and properly identify disputes and then resolve them as expeditiously as possible, we also want to avoid making the same mistakes. I had a boss who loved to remind me that although it's admirable to show that I can put out fires faster and faster, it is much better to find the guy with the matches and get him to stop lighting stuff up! Over time we want to start to see the same types of disputes decrease and eventually go away.

- **Unearned discounts taken:** If we offer discounts to customers for prompt or early payment, then we need to ensure they in fact do pay accordingly. Unfortunately, this is not always the case. Customers frequently take the discount but also pay late. Calculating this and staying on top of this behavior is very important.

Evaluating the Metrics

Arthur and his team had been so busy reviewing operational metrics, they barely noticed the 3 p.m. music. At 3 p.m. each day, a muted yacht rock song starts playing in the hallways of Owens's main office. Today it was "50 Ways To Leave Your Lover." Music at three was the brainchild of the employee wellness committee. The idea is that when you hear the music, you should get up and walk around for 10 minutes. Arthur loved this campaign, because like mosquitoes to a campfire, it drew people to the canteen and the ping-pong table. "Let's stretch our legs," Arthur said nonchalantly. His team exchanged smiles. They knew he was headed straight to the ping-pong table in search of his next victim.

Arthur sat down with Bob, Carol, and Yusef the next morning to share some observations following his review of metrics. The biggest one: he concluded that few people outside of senior finance executives really understand the importance of cash, and they also don't understand how their actions affect Owens's cash flow. "I suggest we add some cash-related metrics to our bonus plan. We'll need to explain and train people so they are prepared to make positive contributions." Carol loved that idea. She pledged to work with the HR team to draw up proposals.

"Yusef, our sales, marketing, and operations teams consistently err on the side of negative forecast bias." Arthur confirmed what Bob and Yusef have known for some time. "We had a couple of stock-outs two years ago because of some hard-to-get switches or something." Bob and Yusef exchanged a knowing glance. Arthur continued, "And now we order on average 10%–15% more than we need of everything. We have enough legacy Titan Motors to meet demand for the next two years, and yet we continue to build them." Yusef did not know about that problem. He looked down at his shoes instead of ahead at his boss. "I suggest we embark on an improved planning process."

"Great idea, Arthur. We are already in motion on that," Yusef said, feeling he needed to redeem himself a bit after the Titan comments.

Arthur continued reading from his notes. "Jeremy does an impressive job holding our suppliers accountable. Quality metrics are at an all-time high. OTIF rates are very impressive, and we can park our cars in the back lot again. But, we don't use those metrics to evaluate our own performance. We are not a very reliable supplier to many of our customers. For sure, we are all over the Mega-Lo-Mart relationship, but I look at our stats with some of our mid-size customers and the story is not so good."

"Just what we need when Worthington is trying to make inroads in that segment," Bob commented. "Yusef, let's get with Jeremy and find a way to implement his supplier metrics, evaluating our performance as a supplier."

"Arthur, that sounds good. But, does that really affect cash?" Carol asked. She wanted to be sure they stay focused on the cash topic.

"Great question, Carol. I believe it really does affect cash. Because we are not all that dependable, our customers have been padding their orders. If they need 10 units a month, they place orders for 12."

"So we are selling more?" Carol asked.

"Not really. We have a dismal OTIF track record, so our sales and marketing team give our customers flexibility to cancel and modify orders on the fly. Our production team can't adjust quickly enough so we keep making too much stuff and still miss our service-level commitments to our customers. They are getting wise. They have 'Jeremys,' too."

"Buy coffee stock," Bob added. The others looked at him confused. "Other Jeremys? I'm picturing an army of over-caffeinated purchasing managers." Bob looked at the forced smiles and brought things back. "Carol, let's have you sit in on this meeting with Jeremy and Yusef as we consider how to better evaluate our performance as a supplier. I suspect there are many other instances of behaviors that cause us to tie up cash and no one is really connecting the dots."

"Lastly, want to talk about Mega-Lo-Mart?" Arthur asked. Bob emitted a soft groan. "We all know that our relationship with Mega-Lo is a bit love-hate. They are one of our largest customers, but they know that. Their commercial terms are some of the most unfavorable we have. For years, I've heard people complain about this and throw hands in air claiming there is nothing we can do."

"Mega-Lo has 90-day payment terms. It's really a problem," Carol interjected, trying to reinforce Arthur's point.

"True, Carol, but did you know our actual collection performance with them is closer to 110 days?"

"So, let me get this straight, Art. They already have the longest payment terms among our customers and then they still pay us 20 days late?" Bob asked.

"Not quite, Bob. The extra 20 days are our fault. On average we cause 20 additional days because of disputes."

"Disputes? What do you mean, Arthur?" Yusef joined the conversation.

"Honestly, I can't give you a simple answer because we don't do a good job identifying and tracking the issues. I pulled a few invoices from last month to try to figure out what is going on. In five cases we forgot to add the correct PO numbers. In six instances we had sent incomplete orders. The killer? I looked back over the past year and found the same errors month after month. In the case of incomplete orders, no one alerted billing. Only until our collection team tried piecing things together did they figure it out. Then it started all over again—month after month."

"Yikes!" Carol interjected, possibly because she saw Bob's face turn red and figured his exclamation would be far more colorful.

"Yikes, indeed," Bob said softly in a defeated tone. "What do we need to do, Art?"

"For starters we need to create a standard set of dispute codes and train those on the front line in how to identify and call out these problems real time. We need to establish a resolution protocol and train the team. Last, we need to hold ourselves accountable to solving the root causes so we avoid them going forward."

The group adjourned and walked out into the hall. Muskrat Love was playing. Bob and Carol headed to the stairs to go to their offices, Yusef went the other direction toward the plant floor, and Arthur made a beeline to the canteen, paddle in hand.

Metrics Best Practices

Here are some best practices to follow:

- Evaluate metrics used by leadership to communicate with the board and investors. Can you see what feeds these metrics? Are there operational indicators (i.e., warning lights) that inform before it's too late? Many of the top-level metrics used at the executive level are after the fact, meaning they are more like the fuel gauge on the car than the speedometer.

- Don't assume that people understand cash flow. Provide training and examples so that teams come to see the importance of maintaining positive cash flow.

(continued)

(*continued*)

- Evaluate operational metrics and ensure they measure the things you really need to measure. For example, Owens was measuring throughput in its billing and collections operations. They focused on how quickly things moved through the cycle versus the effectiveness of the processes. In the scenario described, no one was capturing dispute data nor were they looking for the person with the matches . . . getting them to stop lighting the fires they were trying to put out.

- Consider aligning KPIs and bonuses to cash performance. Be sure, however, that the team understands their role in the process, so they feel empowered to make positive contributions.

Summary

It's quite common that organizations capture all sorts of data and publish a myriad of metrics. But are these measurements linked and do they help promote improvements and more informed decisions? There are sets of metrics that are used by investors to evaluate the overall health of a business, but too often people who can really do something about improving those measures sit within the operations of the business, and their measurements either are not linked or they are not clear enough.

Bob was pleased that he assigned Arthur to review the cash metrics being used at Owens. They now have some tactical plans such as training and alignment of compensation.

8

Resiliency

When Bob started at Owens, the company made only electric motors. They had no retail or consumer business. The motors they made ended up in the products of other mid-size companies. It was a sleepy yet profitable business. There was one production shift from 7 a.m. to 3:30 p.m. Management arrived about 6:30 in the morning and the front offices were empty by 4. Bob, eager to please his leaders, was always first in and last out. . .but that still meant he was home in time to play with his young kids before dinner.

There were few crises to deal with and there was never a need to take work home. That is, until one of Owens's most important customers discovered a major design flaw in the motors they were buying. Jumping at the chance to prove his worth, Bob volunteered to go to the customer, Worthington Tools, to see what the fuss was all about. That's when Bob met Grant.

The Day Grant Became Bob's Mentor

Grant was 10 years his senior and had just been promoted to Worthington's vice president of product development. Worthington Tools had been around for more than 60 years and had an old-school business culture. The head office was not connected to a factory like Owens. Instead, it was nestled into a leafy part of town next to a golf course. The offices had wood paneled walls, working fireplaces, and scary-looking oil portraits of past Worthington executives.

Bob sat for nearly an hour in the reception area waiting on Grant. Finally, he was told to go upstairs to the boardroom. Instead of an informal, initial conversation with a fellow engineer, Bob found himself standing at the entry way of the Worthington boardroom looking out at every member of their executive team. At the other end of the room, seated at the head of a long oak table, was JR Worthington, president and son of the founder.

"Bob! It is Bob, I believe?" JR rhetorically asked in a booming voice. He continued, "Bob, we have a problem. I am told that our metal cutters are not working properly. And, Bob, my name is on those cutters, so it's rather personal for me. Do you understand that, Bob?" Again, a completely rhetorical question. "You see, Bob, my man Grant here says you are the problem. Well, perhaps not you, Bob. But the motors you supply us. They are defective. Our customers don't know the motors are yours. Frankly, they don't care. And, I don't think they should. You agree with me, Bob?"

Still standing because there was no open chair, not that he had the courage to sit down, Bob was frozen. What had he gotten himself into? JR continued for another five minutes before asking Grant to provide a technical assessment for what was going on. This lasted another 20-plus minutes. There was finally a pause.

The silence was worse than the lectures. Bob wasn't at all sure what to say. He was two years out of grad school. Engineering grad school. He had only met in person with two other clients, and they were fellow engineers.

"So you see, Bob, I have this problem. My tools, with my name on it, Bob. My father's name, actually. These tools are failing, Bob. And, Bob, it's your motors that are causing this. I think Grant nicely explained that fact, Bob. I'm sure you agree. So, Bob, the question I am asking, heck the question all of us here at Worthington Tools are asking, Bob, is, well, what are you going to do about it? Bob, what are *you* going to do?" That was the first actual question JR posed and he did so quite loudly and forcibly.

Bob was frozen like a deer staring into the headlights of an oncoming semi-trailer truck.

"Bob? I asked you a question. What are you going to do about these motors? It's my name on the product so I can't have defective metal cutters. So, what's it going to be? What are you going to do?" JR lost all his somewhat folksy dialogue. That's when Grant threw Bob a lifeline.

"JR," Grant said softly and slowly. "Bob and I met earlier today before this meeting. We discussed the problem and agreed on a course of corrective actions. I should have updated you at the start of this meeting. We—Bob and I—fully understand the reputational impact to Worthington. And although the Owens's motors are not identified as such to the end user of our metal cutters, Bob has assured me that they too believe their reputation is also on the line. Bob is, as I understand from the Owens leadership team, their most talented engineer." Bob blushed. He knew the truth and knew that there was no parking space at Owens with his name on it. Grant continued.

"They sent him rather than a salesman or a "handler" because Owens is earnest in wanting to solve this problem and will work with us collaboratively to do so. Bob and I started to map this out before we came in here today." Grant paused, looked over at Bob and gave him a nod. A nod that was a signal to Bob. If you want to get out of this room alive, you better grab the rope I just tossed you; otherwise, JR might use it to hang both of us.

"Uhm, yes. That's right. Owens will solve this. I am sorry, well, actually we—Owens. All of us, including Dan Owens, feel lousy about this. You are right JR, err, Mr. Worthington, sir. We know your name and all. We feel lousy. Yes! Grant, we will work on this and we will get this right!" Despite the word salad that Bob garbled up, his assurance seemed to do the trick. JR stood and simply said, "Well then, men. Go to it! I want to know by the end of the week how this will be fixed and how we will be compensated!"

The Worthington leadership team emptied the cavernous boardroom as quietly as they sat at the table, leaving Grant and a very shaken Bob alone.

"What just happened?"

"I just taught you a lesson, Bob."

"What lesson?" Bob was still trying to process the last hour.

"I believe that we are one of Owens's biggest customers. Is that right?"

"Yes, we really appreciate this . . ." Before Bob could finish, Grant cut him off. He was in no mood for platitudes.

"And you were sent here today because you knew there was a defect in your motors. Am I correct?"

"That is correct," Bob was adapting to the quick pace of questions from this man he had never met and who saved him from the lion's den.

"So, your biggest customer alerts you to a problem. To a defect. They want you to come and discuss it. Yet, you did not prepare. You walked in cold."

"Well, actually I did prepare, Grant. I had our metallurgist explain to me the failure points and . . ." Again, Grant cut him off.

"You didn't bother calling me ahead of the meeting. You didn't ask how high up the ladder at Worthington this problem was being discussed. Had you known that JR Worthington himself was fielding calls from our irate customers, I suspect you would have had reinforcements at a minimum. You walked in cold, and you almost cost your company one of its most important, if not *the* most important, customers. You were completely unprepared."

Bob felt his heart rate increasing and a rush of blood to his face. He had never been spoken to like this. He sailed through college and grad school, winning the admiration of professors and fellow students. At Owens he was something of a golden boy. Sure, there were times of critical feedback, but even those were sandwiched between bits of praise. He didn't know what to say because he realized that Grant was right. He could protest a bit. He was a junior engineer. Wasn't it his boss's fault placing all this responsibility on him? He was not responsible for the Worthington account. Where was the fancy VP of sales that Bob saw driving around in an even fancier car? Wasn't he the guy who should be standing here getting the shellacking?

"I don't know what to say, Grant. You are right. I am unprepared. I am so very sorry."

"And?" Grant prodded. It took Bob a few moments to respond. But he did so carefully.

"Well, I will go straight back to our office and talk with my leadership. I know everyone values this relationship. I'm sure we can find a solution."

"Nope," Grant said without emotion. "That's not good enough, Bob."

"I'm not sure what you want? I'm a junior engineer, Grant. I'm not authorized to make any concessions. I can only pledge that I will give my leadership team a full accounting of the meeting today. They will need to decide how best we respond."

Grant walked across the room, opened the door as if to walk out, but stopped and looked back at Bob. "You see, Bob, I did *my* homework before this meeting. I heard that Owens was sending you. I thought, oh man, you guys don't get it. JR is furious. Sending a junior engineer to deal with something like this? I called some of my contacts at your company. Each one said the same thing. They said Bob is young, but he is bright, creative, and gets things done. You'll be in good hands, Grant, they told me. Were they wrong, Bob?"

Even more flushed, but now slightly annoyed, Bob retorted, "Hey, I said I was sorry. You are right. I should have done homework or whatever. I never said I was from leadership. You made that up in front of your boss. But I said I will go back and tell *my* bosses what is happening. I don't know what more you want from me!"

"Your word. It's your word that I want, Bob. I want you to step up and tell me that you guarantee this problem will be fixed. I don't need a messenger. 'I'll go back and tell my bosses'? If that's all you have to say, we wasted another day. I want your word. Either you can do that, or I was wrong to trust those who told me I was in good hands dealing with you." Grant walked through the door, looked back, and asked, "So, what's it going to be?"

"Yes."

"Yes? What does that mean, Bob?"

"Yes, Grant. The problems with the motors will be resolved, and Owens will ensure that Worthington is satisfied and properly compensated."

"I thought you just told me you are not authorized to commit to that." Grant was taunting him a bit.

"I'm not. I have only my word to offer you. I guess Owens can fire me, Grant. You want my word. You have it."

Grant walked back into the room, stood for a moment or two looking Bob in the eyes, then extended his hand and the two men shook in silence. He smiled and walked out without saying anything else.

This was when Grant became Bob's mentor. It was also the turning point in the business relationship between the two companies. Bob kept his word and got his leadership team to respond in ways that not only satisfied JR but also impressed him. Worthington orders for Owens motors doubled that year.

His leadership recognized the dramatic change in Bob as well. From that day on, he was bolder and more fearless. Grant taught him a career-changing lesson: business is not predictable. There will be good days and bad days. Plans will be made with the best of intentions, but a storm will come along and change everything. In those moments, true leaders will take decisive actions. There won't be time for committees to study and write reports.

Business Is a Live Production: There Are No Do-Overs

In a 2002 *International Herald Tribune* article, Judith Rehak recounted Johnson & Johnson's response to the 1982 Tylenol scare. In a period of a few days, seven people in the Chicago area died after taking Tylenol capsules that were laced with cyanide. At the time, Tylenol was one of the leading pain killers on the market, accounting for roughly 17% of J&J sales. This was not only a public safety crisis but also a public relations nightmare for the company.

James Burke, J&J chairman, made the bold decision to quickly pull all Tylenol product off the shelves in a global recall. Rehak quotes Albert Tortorella, an executive with PR firm Burson-Marsteller, "Before 1982, nobody ever recalled anything. Companies often fiddle while Rome burns."

Burke's decision was not insignificant. The recall and subsequent relaunch cost well over a $100 million.

Resilient organizations need strong leadership, but they also need the capital to respond to rapidly unfolding events. Burke was able to make what is now regarded as one of the best business decisions in the last 50 years because his company could absorb the costs. Resiliency is not just having an umbrella on a rainy day; it's also the ability to quickly take advantage of emerging trends or changes in the market. Think of Apple's ability to continually innovate and offer new products and services. Or Netflix's transformation from a DVD subscription service to a leader in streaming content.

Being resilient requires healthy cash flow. Let's now look at two attributes that help strengthen resiliency:

- Recognition that cash is as important as revenue
- Understanding that there is a big difference between operating cash flow and balance sheet window dressing

Cash and Revenue

Revenue is important, yet there is far too often a fixation on revenue alone. There are many examples of companies that get stuck when markets change, and they simply can't adjust because they don't have the resources (cash) to make necessary investments.

As just noted, Netflix reinvented itself from a DVD by mail business into an entertainment behemoth. By contrast, Blockbuster, once a mighty video rental chain, is now just a distant memory. In an interesting twist of fate, Marc Randolph and Reed Hastings, cofounders of Netflix, offered to sell their fledgling company to Blockbuster for $50 million in 2000, only to be rebuffed because Blockbuster management thought the price was too rich. In 2023 Netflix was worth more than $150 billion. Blockbuster could not react quickly enough to changing technology and customer preferences. Lacking the liquidity to adapt, it filed for bankruptcy in 2010 and by 2014 it closed all its company-owned stores. Strong revenue is not enough to become resilient. It takes cash. Bob saw that firsthand.

How he handled the Worthington problems put Bob on the radar of Owens leadership. He became something of a Mister Fix-it and quickly rose through the ranks, becoming the successor to the founder at a young age. In his first year as president of the Owens Motor Company he pulled his leadership team aside and presented them a bold and frankly audacious plan.

"What is our business?" he asked. After an awkward silence because the question seemed so obvious—the team collectively thought it was a trick question—Yusef replied, "Electric motors. Small ones, big ones, comes in all sorts of colors . . ." The last bit about colors was his attempt at humor.

"I guess that's sort of true. But I think we are in a different business. We make advanced electrical equipment. Right now, it's just motors. But why not generators, power supplies, sensors, and so on? We have the engineering talent and the proven ability to manufacture products. But our real asset is our client base. I'm quite close to the folks at Worthington, as you all know." By now, his response to that crisis is company folklore. "I bet there are no less than a dozen new applications we could provide them. Logic controllers, for example; they source them from all over and frankly struggle with the quality of these sensors. Why aren't we supplying them instead?"

"Aside from the fact that I have no idea what a logical contraption thing is," Carol said wryly.

"Controller. Logic controller," Yusef corrected Carol. She smiled and continued.

"Right. How much will that cost us to develop?"

Bob knew it was a "bet the company decision." It would take millions of dollars and many months before they had a proven technology. They would need to hire more engineers and probably several more expensive salespeople who could sell the new product line. Already bulging at the seams, their one factory had no space to spare. They would need to lease a new building. Carol was right to throw this out as the first question, but she also knew that one day her new, young, and ambitious boss would challenge the status quo and that is precisely why she kept a close watch on their cash flow.

Debt would be expensive and too much leverage could tank the small company. Their stock, although not widely traded, was favored for the generous dividends it paid. If Owens was going to grow, if it was going to keep up with the changing market, it would need capital. Carol understood that and made sure, in those early days, that cash preservation was as important as revenue. She walked the floor of the factory every week, questioning why they had finished products sitting around when almost all their motors were made-to-order. She knew each of their 20 salespeople and kept in close contact, knowing who inflated forecasts and who sandbagged.

Bob's "bet the company" decisions turned out to be a huge success. The company more than doubled in size in four years and then doubled again in the next two years. But with explosive growth came complexity and a passion for chasing revenue. Over time, the focus on cash—on the fundamentals of working capital management—started to wane. Then their second plant had a fire.

Window Dressing

The fire was devastating. Thankfully no one was hurt, but Owens lost tens of millions of dollars of inventory, and the advanced manufacturing lines that built its most in-demand products were damaged beyond repair. They had insurance, but it would take a year or more to recover. A year out of the market gives an opening for nimble competitors to pounce. Bob pressed his team for solutions. How could they act more quickly? Ideas were drawn up but the best one presented was to buy their smaller Dutch competitor, Bakker NV. Bakker's technology lagged Owens, but they had an impressive new factory and a seasoned team of engineers. Bob figured he could cut in half the time it would take to resume production of the Owens line of products. And the Bakker acquisition could help him enter the European market.

There was one, very big problem. Bakker did not want to sell and most certainly did not want to sell to Owens. Two weeks after Bob had his lawyers and bankers approach Bakker with an offer, they came back to him with a blunt answer from Dries Bakker. "We are a growth company. Owens does not have the balance sheet to support our ambitions."

"We've had double-digit growth for the past 18 quarters! What is he talking about?" Bob was both angry and frustrated. Just two months earlier he was featured in an article in a leading business journal that praised his bold management style and Owens's impressive growth. "We created this market! Bakker is only around because they reverse engineer all we do. They are in growth mode? And what does he mean our balance sheet is not strong enough? We've never missed a cash projection since I took the helm!"

Carol hated correcting her boss and even more so in front of others, but Bob was angry, and he wanted answers. "True. We have given analysts forecasts of our cash position each quarter and you are right that we have never missed that guidance. But," she paused, a bit unsure if she should disclose what she was about to say in front of the two bankers and the lawyer in the room. "Maybe we should take this offline Bob. Maybe we can talk about it in private?"

"No time for secrets, Carol! These guys conducted their due diligence. They know our warts and all. Say what's on your mind," Bob said a bit animated.

"In the past six quarters, we met our guidance by mitigating factors, shall we say."

"What does that mean? Mitigating factors? Speak English, Carol!" Animated turned into plain old-fashioned anger.

"We window-dressed, Bob. You know that." Carol now felt defensive. "Last quarter we withheld payments to our vendors. Two quarters ago we asked our copper supplier to delay shipment by a week so we didn't have to take that inventory on our books. We met our guidance because we window-dressed. Dries Bakker is not dumb. When he got an opportunity to look at our books, he put two and two together. Our balance sheet is not as strong as we project."

One of his bankers chimed in. "That's 100% correct. In Europe there are only two suppliers of any size. Dries Bakker knows this. Although his technology is not as advanced as yours, he has ambitions to rapidly expand into Central and Eastern Europe, markets that are growing much faster than the US or Western Europe. A tie-up with Owens will divert precious cash to restarting production of your product lines. And there just isn't enough combined capital between the two companies to do both. Your growth and your products are not the problem, Bob. It's your balance sheet."

Silence.

Bob just got up and walked out of the conference room. He got in his car and drove over to Worthington to talk with Grant.

Bob and Grant had grown very close. They both became presidents of their respective companies about the same time. Worthington was still much bigger, and Grant was older. The mentor dynamic remained even while the two companies became very integrated. Owens was now supplying Worthington with essential sensor technology. It was a very symbiotic relationship. The two men were always candid with each other and there was tremendous trust between the two. Bob wanted to tell Grant about the projected impact in supplying sensors to Worthington and wanted advice on his idea of acquiring Bakker. But before Bob could say anything after the two exchanged in a brief chat about their families, Grant dropped a bombshell.

"Bob, I think I know why you are here. I'd like one of my attorneys to join our conversation, and I must advise you to not disclose anything confidential."

"Grant? It's me. What are you talking about? A lawyer? Are you kidding?"

"Bob, look, I've got a fiduciary responsibility to my company and my shareholders. The fire set you back bigtime. It also will cripple my business if I don't act quickly. My guys tell me it will take you well over a year to resume production. I can't wait that long."

"Grant, I know. I know you will need to find other sources and that we might lose a big portion of our business with Worthington. I don't expect you to wait."

"That's right. We do have back-up plans. But, Bob, these back-up plans are not very good. Your fire exposed a big vulnerability for my company. We will take a big hit this year. There is no good way to tell you this, but we are going to pull sensors in-house."

"What does that mean? Pull in-house?" Bob turned bright red. He knew exactly what it meant.

"We are going into the sensor business, Bob. We'll design and manufacture sensors for our products, and we will also sell them to others. We will be your competitors in this market. You've been a great partner and we will continue to buy your motors but I'm afraid I have no choice. It's a strategic decision for us—one that we need to take."

A week later Bob read the news. Bakker NV to be acquired by Worthington. That same day, Carol sat in his office and briefed Bob on the list of vendors Owens was going to wait two weeks to pay to close the quarter, meeting analyst cash expectations. Bob felt sick. He had a business to rebuild and now a fierce new competitor.

Summary

Resilient organizations are quick to adapt. They have the resources and the culture that enables them to respond to downturns and to capitalize on changing market dynamics. In the Introduction to this book, I referenced a study from Ernst & Young in 2022 that I coauthored. We found empirical evidence linking effective management of cash and working capital to resilience. Simply put, above-average peers (in terms of working capital management) can rebound more quickly from downturns and are better at preserving shareholder value.

But there is a big difference between actual operating cash flow health and window dressing. Because the balance sheet for public companies is reported only on a quarterly basis, it's a snapshot at a point in time. Holding back payments to vendors or temporarily delaying inventory shipments is the equivalent of airbrushing the results. What matters is average daily cash balances. That's cash that can be used to invest in new equipment, pay down debt, and pursue new markets and acquisitions.

Revenue is important, but so is cash. Unfortunately, far too many businesses either don't fully appreciate this or, as was the case with Owens, they lost sight of the basics as they grew, and they only chased revenue. When they most needed cash and a truly healthy balance sheet, they came up short and it took them longer than it needed for them to bounce back from the setback of the fire.

CHAPTER

9

Cash Leadership Office (CLO)

Thoroughly convinced that he needed to shake things up and put a greater focus on cash, Bob sat at his desk looking around his office. Mementos lined the shelves of his bookcase, reminding him of the journey he took to build the company. There is a picture of the first factory, a framed Euro from their expansion into Europe, and a crayon drawing of Bob on a forklift that his granddaughter gave him for Christmas.

For decades he chased increased sales while keeping an eye on expenses. But cash? As he sat there taking it all in, Bob recognized that cash had really been an afterthought. He knew that Carol thought about it. She sees the growing list of capital requirements, but . . . the rest of his executive team? Could he convene a meeting and discuss the importance of focusing on cash? "Is it really that simple?" he said aloud to himself. Do they even know what to do? And what about competing priorities?

Then it came into view in front of him. A photo of Bob presenting Jeremy a silver cup in recognition for driving 15% out of supply costs. Jeremy achieved the impressive results by finding a new supplier in Asia, but this also came with longer lead times and a less predictable schedule. Over the past two years they did save on the cost of the material, but their inventory grew. "Jeremy did what I asked him to do," Bob thought. "So, if I tell everyone to prioritize cash, what other unintended consequences will pop up?"

The past few weeks have been eye-opening. He had great discussions with Jeremy, Yusef, Annette, Caesar, and Mr. Harris, coming away with a new appreciation for the complexity of their jobs. Everyone is trying to do the right thing, but they are optimizing their own departments often at the expense of big-picture goals. Owens has never really held these executives responsible for cash and Bob knew that if that is to change, he would have to first give them the tools and training.

Most businesses have organized based on the P&L and often operate in silos. Therefore, a bold undertaking will be required to develop a cash culture, where cash decisions are considered in equilibrium with other priorities such as sales growth, customer service, and profit margin.

Developing a Cash Culture

Bob serves on the board of St. Luke's Hospital with Naomi. She is the CEO of Tri-Plast, a chemical company, and she told Bob some time ago that she had formed a cash leadership office (CLO) that has been quite successful. He realized later that he had not really paid much attention to what she was telling him at the time because he has a bias against things that sound consult-ant-y. CLO? Sounds like something a newly minted MBA might present to him. But as he sat there in the quiet of his office, he wondered if he was too dismissive of ideas like this. Tri-Plast has been very successful, consistently beating analyst forecasts. And they are frequently lauded for their ability to generate cash from operations. A CLO? Hmmm. Bob picked up his phone. "Hello? Naomi? It's Bob. Any chance I can buy you lunch next week?"

As Bob would discover talking with Naomi, creating a cash culture in an organization takes a good deal of focus and effort. Most organizations have long ignored the balance sheet and have set up metrics and KPIs that can conflict with the preservation of cash. A CLO can help an organization identify opportunities to improve. I like to refer to this as the art of the possible. How effective and efficient can an organization be at generating and preserving cash from operations? There are seven important aspects of this approach:

- **Strategy alignment:** Review capital requirements of the business and how much cash it will need, taking into account headwinds it might face.

- **Opportunity identification:** In order to meet the cash needs, what actions need to be taken?

- **Initiative management:** Follow-through is something most organizations struggle with. It's vital that the initiatives deliver the forecasted value creation on time and on budget.

- **Metrics and reporting:** Ensure that the right things are being measured and that stakeholders and leadership have the reports they need to drive change.

- **Incentives:** Adjust compensation and incentives to drive desired behaviors.

- **Training and communication:** Don't assume the team knows what to do or why the business is changing.

- **Business operating model:** Ultimately, the goal is to embed this new approach into the business operating model.

Sunsetting CLO

Arriving at Tri-Plast early, Bob was surprised to see Naomi in the lobby ready to greet him. "Good morning, Naomi. Thank you so much for meeting with me today. I know you are extremely busy."

"For you, Bob, I will always find the time." She led him across the lobby to a large conference room. The walls were lined with patents Tri-Plast owns.

Bob had been in this room for hospital board events and understood why Naomi likes to bring visitors there. The many framed patents underscore the reputation Tri-Plast has for innovation. He knows that Naomi deserves much credit for this because she is very creative and pushes everyone around her to challenge assumptions. This meeting will be good, Bob thought. If anyone can change his mind, Naomi probably has the best shot. Bob knows that Owens needs to do something to change course, but does it really need another project management office? That's what this CLO thing sounds like to him. Yet another committee or special group. "I keep hearing about the CLO thing. I know you told me about it a year or so ago. I'm not convinced." Bob started things off rather defensively.

Naomi took it in stride, laughed, and punched right back: "Okay. I see, Bob. It's now *my* job to sell you on something that will help your business and benefit your shareholders? Sit down and I will tell you our story."

"Listen, I, too, thought we could just set targets for the business and then hold people accountable. Why do we need to establish some new structure? We have highly motivated—and highly compensated—executives who should be able to move the needle. And that's exactly all we ever accomplished. We just moved the needle a bit. Somehow, we could not accomplish a step change. The business was too far away from being a true cash culture. Frankly, we didn't know what we didn't know."

"I get that, Naomi. I've been having discussions with my leadership team for the past few weeks and as we talk about what needs to be done, the elephant in the room is always: How did we get here? Why is it so hard to instill solid cash management principles?"

Naomi replied, "Yep. We asked the same questions at Tri-Plast. Then one day, a board member sent me an article about how some organizations are applying concepts to cash management similar to zero-based budgeting (ZBB). Are you familiar with ZBB, Bob?"

"I think so, Naomi, but please explain."

"Well, to simplify, ZBB requires that budgets are based on what is needed for the business rather than incremental increases or decreases. Each year, the budgets start at zero and then get built up. As I read the article, a light bulb went off. Can we apply similar concepts for cash and capital? The status quo approach is reliant on making incremental improvements. Can we shave a day or two off DSO? Can we find a way to reduce inventory by 5% next year? This sort of approach moved the needle, but it didn't really transform. Further, I saw that as we improved one aspect of our business another unit degraded."

"Naomi, I think they call that whack-a-mole."

"You are bringing me back to my Wisconsin State Fair days, Bob," Naomi chuckled. "And that's a great way to describe what we experienced. The fact is—no matter how earnestly folks were at addressing cash management, we just didn't have the data or controls to make a sustainable transformation. Business units could not fully see the impact of their day-to-day decisions and, frankly, we sent mixed messages by how we managed and incentivized them. We needed to do something different. That's why we established a CLO."

"Okay, you've piqued my interest, Naomi. Can I meet with your team in the CLO?"

"Nope," Naomi quickly replied.

Bob looked confused and a bit irritated. Owens and Tri-Plast don't compete, and he always valued his friendship with her.

Naomi saw his reaction, smiled, and then continued. "We dismantled our CLO a few months back. When we started this journey three years ago, we always had the goal that the CLO should sunset. We recognized the need to do something quite different and dramatic, but we also wanted to find ways to bake this into our business operating model. We needed a focused approach to help us make the step change—and we needed to also identify the changes required to make this new way of life sustainable. In some cases that meant we had to change operating models and organization design. We had to challenge our assumptions regarding talent and whom we needed in key roles. We modified our metrics and incentives and transformed operations reviews."

Bob was coming around. When people discussed this concept with him, he always bristled at the thought of creating another bureaucracy. Hearing that the CLO could—and as Naomi said, should—sunset appealed to him greatly.

"Bob, you can't talk with our CLO team, but you can talk with Meredith, whom I tasked with setting it up, managing it, and then disbanding it. Meredith was the perfect choice for this effort. She ran our financial planning and analysis function. She is well respected across the business, knowing where the bodies are buried—so to speak. We knew that if we were going to do this right and get the results we needed, this had to be her full-time job. We also decided early on that we would give our board of directors progress updates at each meeting. Bob, are you familiar with the concept of "burning the ships in the harbor"?

"Something you did at the Wisconsin State Fair?" Bob quipped and then continued, "I believe it means no turning back.

In military campaigns, invaders would burn the ships in the harbor on arrival to force the soldiers to fight it out. Is that right?"

"Exactly! We decided to take that approach. We told the board that over the course of the next few years we would fundamentally change the way we managed cash. We invited them to quiz us and hold us accountable. For this, we needed a strong dedicated leader. And Meredith did not let us down. Our board took note, analysts have commented on our substantial progress, and the results are apparent when we measure shareholder return. Meredith got promoted to boot!"

A devious smile swept across Bob's face. Before he could say anything, Naomi added, "And we awarded Meredith incentives to stay with Tri-Plast. No poaching, Bob! But I will play poker with you any time you want."

"Before I introduce you to Meredith, let me tell you how we presented this to the board." Naomi connected her laptop computer to the projector and brought up a presentation. "As said, Bob, the leadership team locked arms and decided we were going to burn the ships in the harbor. We anticipate many changes coming our way—some we already know about, such as new competitors and regulatory changes, and many we were sure we would encounter, but we didn't have clear visibility in how it would affect Tri-Plast. For example, five years ago we were the clear market leader in Brazil. We knew that some of our Asian competitors were starting to make inroads, and because that is an important market, we had to invest in order to stay competitive. That meant we had to increase our capex in Brazil by 300%. When we started to discuss this with our board they challenged us to think more comprehensively. They wanted us to discuss scenarios—positive and negative—that would affect our cash and capital allocation." Naomi flipped to the first slide that said *Strategy*.

Establishing the CLO

- **Strategy:** The first step to creating a cash culture is mapping out what the cash needs will be going forward. Sadly, most businesses start with their current operating cash performance and then someone in finance asks operational stakeholders if they can improve by a certain percentage. Can we shave a few days off inventory? Think we can collect a bit faster? This approach is not at all transformative.

  I am proud of the fact that I've run three marathons considering that when I decided to enter my first one, I was only running a mile or two at a time. If I started with a one-mile run and then said to myself, "I bet I can increase that by 10% this year," I would never have finished the race. Instead, I started with the strategy: I want to successfully run 26.2 miles in the next 12 months. To do that, I had to make a lot of changes. I had to stick to a disciplined training strategy, had to improve my diet and even had to go to bed early on Friday nights so I could do long running training on Saturdays.

  Similarly, if we identify the capital we will need, the debt we have to repay, headwinds we foresee as inflation increases, we can then start the discussion with a strategic target.

- **Opportunity identification:** Once we know our cash needs via our strategy alignment, we then need to find ways to fund. Give the CLO the tools and resources needed to conduct analysis. We spoke of doing SKU-level analysis in Chapter 5 of this book. This sort of in-depth review will facilitate fact-based discussions and help prioritize improvements. This should include other areas, such as tax, licenses, real estate, and benefits funding.

  Create common charters for the initiatives so that progress can be tracked. There should be benefit measurement milestones and mitigation plans if teams fail to meet the targets. Pay close attention to establishing a baseline at the start of the initiative and ensure the way it will be measured translates into cash. For example, in Chapter 6, Caesar and Rohit created an initiative to improve the planning process. They estimated that these efforts would generate $10 million of reduced inventory. The CLO charter should note the baseline from which that inventory reduction will be measured. What if there is a strategic decision to build another $20 million of inventory to meet an anticipated surge in demand? Will we be able to see if Caesar's program generated the anticipated results?

- **Metrics and reporting:** We discussed in Chapter 7 how critical it is to align metrics and use them to drive results. More is not always better. The CLO will need to continue what Arthur started and roll out meaningful metrics and KPIs. The senior leadership team, such as Bob and Carol, don't need the same level of detail as Jeremy, but the data should all roll up. At the Bob-Carol level, they will need to see how well the business units are doing according to plan. When there are variances (positive or negative) they will need data to understand why and what possible mitigation efforts will be taken.

- **Incentives:** The CLO should review compensation incentive packages and recommend to leadership ways to better align. In Chapter 2 we discussed the idea of paying sales commissions only on cash collected versus signed contracts. We want the compensation to drive intended outcomes.

- **Communication and training:** This is one area almost all organizations shortchange and then really regret doing so later. The team needs to know why we are doing things differently and how they fit into the effort. This must be reinforced several times in order for it to be absorbed. Even finance teams below the senior leaders often don't really understand cash levers. The CLO needs to develop and implement robust change management programs if we want to sustain results.

- **Business operating model:** Opinions differ on this, but I have the pen and it is my book—so I'm advancing my opinion! I think an effective CLO should work itself out of business in three to five years. We really want the business to put cash on equal footing with cost and revenue. To do that will require a lot of effort. Bob has come to see that continuing to do things the same way or even with some incremental change will not create a cash culture at Owens. But, he is also right to want the new strategy, processes, metrics, and so on to be fully integrated into the business operating model.

Different Ways to Burn the Ships in the Harbor

Naomi paused from reviewing these key elements with Bob. "What do you say we now go meet the real brains of the operation?"

"Meredith?" Bob asked. "I'd love to meet her."

Naomi asked Meredith to explain to Bob how Tri-Plast set up the CLO. They gave a lot of consideration to what would work best in their corporate culture. For example, funding and how the CLO will interact with operating leaders is really important to iron out at the start. Meredith explained to Bob the four options they considered:

- **Directed centralized:** This is the strongest form of CLO. A centralized core team commissions analysis of the business and not only sets targets but also creates and manages project charters. They assemble resources to help business units and provide a central source of funding. Tri-Plast used this model because they wanted to achieve maximum results in a concentrated period. They recognized at the outset that a model like this requires a strong leader—Meredith—as well as active support and air cover from the CFO, CEO, and board. This is truly a burn-the-ships-in-the-harbor approach and one that is highly visible throughout the organization.

- **Autonomous decentralized:** At the other end of the extreme is an approach that is decentralized and autonomous. A skeletal CLO team sets cash targets but allows the business units to decide how to achieve the results, creating their own projects. They must self-fund and assign their own resources. This approach works only in organizations that are already quite mature. It's a small step from status quo and incremental change because it just creates a high-level awareness of the need for improvement, without providing the tools or resources often necessary.

- **Autonomous centralized:** With a bit more structure and providing project management resources, the autonomous centralized model sets the targets but also helps business units establish project charters and provides project management resources. Business units still need to decide how to go after the improvements and must still provide funding. This works for organizations set up as holding companies that have a very hands-off and small central management team. Unlike autonomous decentralized, this does recognize the need for some central support and management.

- **Directed decentralized:** This is closest to what Tri-Plast implemented but leaves some of the ships in the harbor. This CLO provides analysis, sets targets, commissions charters, but then leaves day-to-day project management to the business units. Some centralized budget is allocated, but it lacks the full-on force of a directed centralized effort. For this option to work, each business unit needs to have strong "Merediths" driving results.

In considering which model works best for achieving results, leaders also need to consider which will be most effective at ensuring sustainability and allowing the CLO to sunset. A burn-the-ships-in-the-harbor approach is highly visible. It requires full support and buy-in from leadership and a strong, dedicated manager to implement and run. Yet this approach will generate the most transformative results at the quickest pace. It acknowledges that investments must be made and resources allocated to training, change management, and communication, ensuring sustainability.

Although a toe in the water approach is easiest to start, it is also easiest to set aside. It really comes down to how committed leaders are to establishing a cash culture. I recall two failed attempts on my part to run a marathon. Then I decided to burn the ships. I told everyone that I was training and would run the Chicago marathon that year. I had only one option to avoid embarrassment. I did follow through, and I ran two more after that.

CLO Best Practices

Here are some best practices to follow:

- Get consensus from the C-suite leadership team: if you truly want to create a cash culture, generating transformational results that are sustainable, then you must be aligned and commit to the journey ahead.

- Take an honest assessment of your organizational readiness for a CLO effort. Are you willing and able to burn the ships in the harbor or do you need to proceed more cautiously and take an incremental approach?

- Identify a leader who can run the CLO. This person should be well respected by the business and know how to drive results. It's an ideal job for an executive who likes a good challenge and can be a perfect opportunity for them to demonstrate their leadership capabilities to the C-suite and board.

- Plan for controversy and trade-off decisions. Ensure that the CEO and CFO provide air cover to the CLO team and discuss in advance how to manage through difficult situations.

- Consider at the start setting a timer for the CLO. True transformation will take at least three years, but likely should be wrapped up within five years. A preset timer helps advance a sense of urgency.

- Don't skimp on training, communication, and change management. Making one-time improvements that are not sustainable is counterproductive. Be sure that your team has the tools and resources to chase continuous improvements.

- Evaluate business reporting and metrics, aligning KPIs and incentives with your cash goals.

Summary

In summary, corporate cultures take shape and calcify over years. Because most organizations have historically been more focused on revenue growth, profitability, and customer service, cash considerations are frequently an afterthought. Bringing about changes beyond incremental and ensuring that the changes are sustainable will likely require a concentrated intervention through the formation of a cash leadership office. Ideally the CLO will have a mandate from the C-suite and possibly the board and will be given the resources, budget, and authority to harvest results and develop a cash culture. With an eye on sustainability, the CLO often has a sunset provision and works toward integrating new operating protocols into the business operating model. And, like most corporate change initiatives, the selection of the CLO leader is vital to its success. Find your Meredith and back her up.

CHAPTER

10

Nonmanufacturing Examples

"Alright, ladies, it's time to move north from Texas. How about the next few rounds we play Omaha Hold 'em?" Carol loved these nights playing cards with four of her closest friends. They met in college or shortly after and each woman has pursued careers with great passion.

Makayla and Carol met freshman year. Both had very odd roommates and they quickly bonded in the dorm study lounge telling each other one story after another. They would laugh until late in the night. Carol was an accounting major and Makayla was following in the footsteps of her mother for a career in medicine.

"I'm going to need to see your cash up front, Carol. Big-wig corporate finance types just love to take advantage of simple country doctors like me!" The women laughed at what had become a running joke. Each was very successful in her chosen career, and each tried to outdo the others playing it down.

Makayla was not a country doctor. She was chief of surgery at St. Luke's Hospital.

This was a power gathering. In years past the women met more frequently; now it was once a quarter. Cards, pizza, martinis, and camaraderie with other successful women who understand the pressures and responsibilities that come when people describe you as a *first* . . . such as the first woman chief of surgery or the first managing partner of the largest law firm in the state. They understood the milestones they had achieved and had done so because many others before them made it possible, but they wanted to be known for their achievements beyond being a *first*.

Very much like the bonding years earlier over odd roommates, Makayla found another kindred soul in Mia as they struck up a conversation at a local coffee shop, popular with grad students. Mia's parents were both attorneys and the women shared their excitement yet reticence of selecting the same career paths that their parents forged.

Paulette gave up a career in law to start a fashion business. She and Mia were a year apart at the same law school. To the great surprise of her classmates, Paulette, the top student in her class, traded a job at a white-shoe law firm to open a retail business, selling apparel to petite women. "You must be joking!" Mia asked in shock when Paulette told her of the plans years ago. "You know you will easily make partner?" Paulette knew that, but also thought that at its dawn, this new thing—the internet—might be a good platform for retail, especially if it was geared to meeting a real need with a targeted audience. Last fall, Paulette flew her friends to Paris fashion week on her private jet. Her bet paid off.

And then there was Grace. The other women, extroverts, had big personalities. No one at Owens second-guessed who the finance chief was. At St. Luke's, Makayla was not only chief of surgery but also sat on the board of directors. And Paulette had been on the cover of so many business and trade magazines that her friends stopped cutting them out and sending them to her with notes of congrats. Grace, by contrast, was very quiet and relished sitting back and taking it all in. This has led several to underestimate her at their peril.

Grace inherited a construction business that her grandfather started. She spends her days in jeans and a hard hat and commands respect in an old-boy world. In the industry she is known for her attention to detail, razor-sharp decision-making ability, and nerves of steel. No one pushes her around. There are the occasional clueless men who think Grace is just a trust fund woman who relies on others to run the business. She loves those encounters. Her team will cringe as if watching a slow-motion car wreck. Luring them in with seemingly basic questions, the men start to think they were right with their preconceived assessment. Then, without seeing it coming, they will find themselves backed into a corner unable to answer her questions. She is quiet and observant and masterful at leading her company.

"So, Carol, I ran into Bob at the Chamber dinner last week. He was going on and on about how you are really turning things around at Owens. Something about a cash leadership office? Will you tell us more?" Grace asked.

"Ha! Next time you see my boss tell him flattery doesn't pay the bills. I'd rather have a bonus."

Grace knew that Carol was joking, but she did in fact talk to Bob at length about the transformation and being the shrewd businessperson, she wanted to see if there were good ideas she could apply at Lambert Construction. "I saw the new Mercedes out front. I'm pretty sure you aren't going through the Sunday papers cutting coupons." For Grace to use sarcasm, Carol recognized she was earnest in wanting to know more about the focus on cash that Bob mentioned.

"Well, I'm not sure where to start. Without disclosing too much, we realized that with our expansive growth we sort of took our eyes off the balance sheet. We allowed working capital to grow and our operating cash flow was not in synch with our revenue growth."

"Ladies, I might just learn something useful tonight. And I seldom think that after wasting a few hours with you!" Makayla said playfully. "We have massive capital projects at the hospital and our cash flow is not keeping up. We are getting squeezed on all fronts. Let's order those pizzas and, Carol, will you please give us a crash course on cash management?"

Cash Management in Various Industries

To my readers who work in manufacturing companies or invest in them, please recognize that I spent nine chapters explaining cash and working capital management in terms that will likely seem quite familiar. However, my readers who work in a law firm, at a hospital, or in retail are the real heroes. If you made it this far in the book, you showed tremendous patience. Thank you for hanging in there. This chapter is dedicated to you.

Cash is universally king, but the levers will be different depending on the type of organization. Let's explore those differences in this chapter. We will look at four different types of entities:

- Retailers
- Construction-related businesses
- Professional services firms
- Health care providers

Retailers

In most retail businesses the merchants are the team quarterbacks. They make very big bets on what will sell, often investing large amounts of capital up-front. When they get it right, the margins on retail merchandise can be quite high and the business is very profitable. But recall our previous discussion about inventory. Every dollar invested has equal value, although it most likely doesn't generate equal returns. Retail segments such as apparel can be high-wire acts given the fickle nature of fashion trends. Skinny jeans are in fashion one day and out the next. Effective merchandise inventory management must be a core competency for retail businesses. They also must closely manage their supply relationships.

Unless the merchant is selling commodities, where there are several opportunities to switch sources, they will need to form and maintain close relationships with their suppliers. That is not to mean they don't have leverage over the suppliers; instead, they need to understand the type of leverage and impact.

For example, Mega-Lo-Mart is one of the largest discount retailers in the country. They account for 50% of Owens's consumer power generator sales. That gives Mega-Lo-Mart tremendous influence and power over how Owens prices, packages, and distributes the products. It also can influence other commercial arrangements such as payment terms, OTIF (on-time—in-full) requirements, and so on. But Mega-Lo-Mart also needs to walk a fine line to ensure the relationship is mutually beneficial. Owens's products are well-known brands and are valued by consumers. Mega-Lo-Mart doesn't want to drive Owens into unsustainable arrangements.

This sort of symbiotic relationship affects most sectors, but it does have unique attributes in retail. The retailers gather a significant amount of consumer purchasing data that can be very useful to suppliers. And, likewise, suppliers can help their retail partners stay ahead of trends and changing consumer preferences that can play a big role in pricing and mark-down strategies. When this becomes formalized, the retailer and the vendor enter into joint business planning.

Because most retail sales are "cash" sales, they often don't carry much in the way of accounts receivable. By cash I mean that the transaction is settled at the time of purchase. Customers pay for what they are buying at that point, unlike in a business-to-business context where the buyers are invoiced and have a predetermined period to pay. The retailer may, of course, offer their own credit cards and accept that as a form of payment. In almost all cases, those cards are issued by banks and the banks hold those transactions on their balance sheets. (Even if the card looks like it is just a Mega-Lo-Mart card—odds are a banking partner issues and manages the cards.)

So, to effectively manage cash, retailers need to be laser focused on managing their inventory and their supply relationships. Let's now consider some key concepts that affect how they do that:

- **Assortment:** This refers to merchandise the retailer decides to carry. It can be greatly affected by seasonality, demographics, and customer preferences. It's also reflective of the type of retail business they aim to be and the brand they convey in the market. Some aspects of assortment management include the following:
  - **Market demand:** Retailers either chase demand or create demand. Both strategies have pros and cons. If demand already exists, then the retailer can tap into that and offer merchandise that satisfies. But if other retailers are offering the same merchandise, then they must differentiate their offerings. This can be done by price (which might negatively affect margin) or convenience, such as always being in stock for popular items or having many locations so buying is quick and convenient. This requires capital investment in buying more stock and possibly maintaining

more locations. Another common point of differentiation is experience. Perhaps they offer free parking, personal shoppers, unconditional return policies, or even live piano recitals. Again, this takes capital investment to support these enhanced experiences.

> Before I discuss demand creation, I want to acknowledge that I'm talking mostly of brick-and-mortar retailers. Those with physical locations. Later in this section I will discuss e-commerce.

Creating demand can offer real advantages. If Lord's Department Store is the only place to buy a certain brand and that brand becomes popular, then the retailer can be more selective in capital investments and will have greater control over pricing strategy. This concept is quite popular in a segment referred to as "fast fashion," in which offerings are limited and turn over quickly. This encourages the buyer to act now; otherwise, the item might not be available in the future. Most often, the supply chain is vertically integrated. The designers, merchants, and sourcing teams are all part of one team under one roof. They spot emerging trends, decide on how much to allocate to that trend, design the items, find manufacturers to produce—often in limited runs—and then sell through without a lot of additional replenishment. On to the next trend.

But this strategy requires merchants to truly be on top of or ahead of consumer preferences. They still must make bets, but if the bets go wrong, there might not be a safety net that comes with an already known brand or designer. Again, pros and cons associated with chasing and creating demand.

- **Category management:** If you sell razors, you need to sell blades, and vice versa. Some categories require ancillary or supporting merchandise that a business might not otherwise stock. Understanding the full category and what is appealing to the shopper can be something of an art and separates good merchants from the rest. Often the merchant has a shopper in mind and will specify a basket of offerings that together promote more sales. This is the 1 + 1 = 3 concept. Having a mix of merchandise will promote higher overall sales and reduce margin erosion from markdowns. As you might guess, this requires wise investment decisions. Capital is limited—there is only so much that can be invested and, as said, each investment dollar is worth the same. The art and science is to maximize the return on those investment dollars.

- **Life cycle management:** What is hot or in demand today will fade over time. There are few offerings that hold consistent demand over time. Well, perhaps that is overstating things. Many items will eventually plateau if the demand does not go away altogether. I'm guessing in the decades that followed Ezra Warner's invention of the manual can opener in 1858 sales of the new contraption grew steadily. We still buy can openers today and although I don't have current demand data, I'll bet you a donut and coffee that demand has plateaued. Not a lot of excited rushes to go out and buy one.

  Closely monitoring demand variations is key to effectively managing the life cycle of merchandise. In addition to the natural ebb and flow of demand, seasonality and special events can spike demand. During hurricane season, plywood, bottled water, and batteries spike in coastal regions. The market for a dozen roses quickly declines after Valentine's Day.

> I think there might be an opportunity for a new market—
> "I love you so much I missed Valentine's Day *on purpose* so
> I could buy you three times the number of flowers!" What
> do you think?

- **Space optimization/visual requirements:** Assortment mix can also be influenced by the size of the physical store. If there is too much space and too few items on display, that might work for an ultra-hip, trendy designer but for almost everyone else it will cheapen the shopping experience. This goes hand in hand with category management. The shopper wants options and variety. A space that is too spartan signals a lack of options. Conversely, spaces that are overcrowded with too much stuff can also cheapen the experience. If the store is too busy and chaotic, it's hard for shoppers to find what they want.

  This is a big problem for the retail industry in North America right now. There is an oversupply of retail space relative to demand. Certainly, e-commerce has driven much of this shift, but we have also gone through fundamental shifts in shopping preferences. Big indoor malls anchored by big department stores are nowhere nearly as popular as they were a decade ago. Chain stores added locations to the point of diminishing returns. So, retailers are sitting on too much space and are challenged with how best to fill those spaces in ways that generate increased sales.

- **Replenishment:** The concepts just discussed affect replenishment strategies. Monitoring changes in demand and category requirements must be considered when replenishing inventory. If merchandise is on a downward demand curve, we don't want to replenish at the same rate as when it was ascending. We might hold some items that help the overall category sales but the sale of some of those individual items should not trigger an automatic replenishment. There are many data-analytic offerings in the market to assist buyers with this critical task. As said at the start, effective retailers recognize that merchandising assortment and replenishment is really at the heart of what they must do effectively.

Where and how merchandise is replenished is important. Perhaps it is sent directly from the vendor or drop-shipped to the store location. Maybe all the replenished items are sent to a central warehouse the retailer maintains and then shipped to the store as needed. The service levels assigned to these stock keeping units drives a lot of these decisions. If the item is highly in demand and stocking out the retailer must replenish faster to avoid lost sales.

- **Pricing strategy:** This affects just about every sector and is not unique to retail. However, pricing strategy does have some unique requirements in retail that are not as pronounced in a business-to-business market. In an ideal world, every dollar invested in merchandise yields high rates of return and does so quickly. We don't live in such a world. If merchandise is moving slowly, then discounts are often the mechanism to stimulate demand. Let's say we bought 100 Owens Mini home generators at $350 per unit and are selling them for $700 each. We sell 30 at that price but it has taken months. We reduce by 20% to $540 and sell another 50. But sales again plateau. Although we still have 20 left, we've recouped our $35,000 investment and made a 37% return on the investment. Are we excited? Well . . . it depends.

How long did these sales take? There is a time value to money. How was the return on other things we were selling? (Every invested dollar costs the same but doesn't always have the same rate of return.) Did we give up valuable floor space that could have been assigned to faster-moving, more profitable items? Did we have to incur extra costs associated with the markdown such as advertising? What do we do with the remaining 20 generators? If we do a final markdown sale, do we hurt our goodwill with the shoppers who bought it at full price? Do we train them to wait until we offer sales and inevitably offer discounts? And in the case of our branded merchandise, do we erode the brand premium? All these decisions have significant impact on how a retailer manages inventory.

There are other situations like certain buy-one-get-one offerings (commonly referred to as BOGO) that can spike sales but can create artificial or non-sustainable demand signals. Pricing strategy is the third leg of the retailer's core competency stool, the other two being assortment and replenishment.

- **E-commerce/omnichannel:** So, it turns out this thing called the internet might be here to stay. I suspect that most of us increased our use of e-commerce during the pandemic. We have grown accustomed to how easy it is to find exactly what we want and then quickly compare prices. It's not just price that influences how or where we shop online. The ease of navigating websites, return policies, and how quickly our purchased goods are shipped also have an influence.

Retailers who operate physical stores and a presence online are described as being omnichannel because they reach buyers in many ways. Operating in an omnichannel environment does have unique demands on assortment and replenishment strategies.

If inventory is held centrally, then perhaps regional or seasonal impacts become less pronounced, and the retailer can offer a wider assortment than they can via physical stores. But, the last-mile delivery shifts from the shopper to the retailer. In the brick-and-mortar environment, the shoppers come from many different locations (homes) to a relatively small number of locations (stores) and then take their purchases back to their homes. In an e-commerce world, the retailer now must find a way to send merchandise directly to the shopper. Although fixed store overhead costs go down, transportation and packaging costs go up. There is a trade-off. This also might affect how shoppers make buying decisions. If they are in the store, they might be tempted by other offerings on display or might decide to buy three of the things they know they need/want at once to avoid another trip to the store. But, on the internet, they can likely get each item one at a time. Of course, there might be some incentives on bundling to avoid shipping costs, but trends are moving more toward free shipping for every item.

In fulfilling these orders, the retailer might do some from a central location but might also fulfill via their store network. Replenishment signals based on how this fulfillment is being arranged need to be monitored closely.

Returns can also complicate inventory holdings. Let's say I buy a heavy down feather winter coat via the e-commerce portal from Lord's Department Store. I have it sent to my home in Phoenix because I'm planning a trip to Minneapolis in a week. The trip gets canceled, I no longer need/want the coat, so I drive over to their Scottsdale location and return it. Now they have one heavy down feather coat that might never sell in Arizona. This example is a bit simplistic, but big retailers struggle with the mismatch that can occur when merchandise is bought online and returned to physical locations.

Construction-Related Businesses

The biggest differences between the manufacturing case study we reviewed in the first nine chapters of this book and construction-related businesses has to do with contract management, billing, and collections.

> I'm using *construction-related* to include a broad range of businesses that get paid based on implementation or completion. For example, this might include IT, consulting firms, companies that build and install manufacturing equipment, and of course, those that build buildings.

Most construction-related contracts are set up with milestone billing. This means the provider can bill the buyer according to agreed-on completion milestones. There are several big situations that arise that can affect cash:

- **Nebulous language in acceptance terms:** Far too often contracts will have provisions that allow for the buyer to sign off on completion based on markers such as satisfaction. If the language is too vague, leaving too much room for different interpretations, this can prevent the provider from issuing and collecting these milestone payments. Spending time up-front to clarify the conditions and ways to measure will pay off down the road.

- **Issuing bills:** In the case of milestone billing, it often requires project managers to stay on top of the completion dates and issue the invoices on time. I've yet to come across a construction-related business where they do this smoothly. Either they get tripped up on nebulous language or they simply don't complete the supporting documentation in time. There are software applications that can aid with this but holding project managers accountable via their performance compensation will have a big impact. When the airlines started to measure on-time departures and hold gate agents and ground crews accountable, on-time departures soared. In a similar way, it's vital to ensure project managers make sure that invoices are submitted as soon as a milestone is completed and that all the supporting documentation is in place.

- **Liens:** These are claims a contractor can file to encumber the project if the payer is late or fails to meet obligations. This can tie up the title to the project and acts as a powerful tool to force payment. Lien provisions are written into contracts up-front. Sending notice threatening the invocation of a lien if payments are seriously delayed can often do the trick before a formal lien is filed.

  The construction sector tends to include subcontractors and providers who really struggle with cash because they frequently need to buy expensive materials up-front. This creates a bit of "rob Peter to pay Paul" syndrome. It's therefore common to see pay-when-paid language in agreements. I'll pay you for the portion of the project when I get paid. This creates an interdependency between parties.

Professional Services Firms

The only real distinctions that might differ from approaches we have already discussed have to do with billing as well as the form of accounting treatments.

> I am not a CPA nor will I ever attempt to provide accounting advice.

Smaller partnerships and limited liability corporations often use cash basis accounting versus accrual accounting. And the high-level difference between the two is this: With cash accounting, the transaction is recorded when cash comes in or goes out the door. In accrual accounting, revenue is recognized at the time of sale (not when the actual cash is collected) and expenses are recorded when they are incurred (not when they are actually paid). Cash accounting is a more simplistic form of accounting and tends to be used by small companies, but some large professional services firms that don't sell products and therefore don't have inventory or accumulated accounts payable also use cash basis accounting. The reason I call this out: those that do use cash basis accounting should be hyper-motivated to collect cash, particularly if income distribution is based on this.

Mia's law firm uses cash basis accounting because there are tax advantages associated with not recognizing all the work in progress versus the actual cash collected. However, she and her partners are distributed a portion of the profits each year and that comes from the pool of cash on hand.

Hence, for any professional services firm or those that use cash accounting: it's even more important to the partners (or those whose earnings depend on the distribution of cash on hand) to ensure timely billing and collections. Although lawyers and consultants don't want to be bothered with billing and collections, it's really in their best interests to be very involved.

Health Care Providers

Hospitals and clinics are often massive and sprawling enterprises. They consume capital at voracious rates and have all the same fundamental working capital concerns as companies like Owens. Hospitals have inventory and fixed assets. They buy a lot so there are very complex procurement processes. They have a large customer base (patients) and a large workforce. Keeping control over inventory, procurement, and capital investments is a focus they share with other sectors we've already discussed in this book. There is one very big distinction that has a tremendous impact on cash: the way their customers (patients) pay them. This is referred to as revenue cycle management (RCM).

Entire books are written on RCM so this will just be a very high-level overview to give the reader a sense of the complexity of the process. Most patients receiving care have some form of insurance (private or from the government). Of course, there are some with no insurance as well. Let's focus on those insured as they make up the vast majority. RCM has several different stages:

- **Patient intake:** You go to a doctor's office, clinic, or even urgent care and before you can settle into an uncomfortable chair and read a three-year-old magazine, you are presented a stack of paperwork. This intake process is the first step because the provider needs to capture critical information about your health, for sure, but also about your insurance. Even before care is provided, the billing process has started.

- **Eligibility verification:** Once the provider has your insurance information, they need to verify what type of plan you have and what it will or will not cover. Four common types of plans are:
  - **Health maintenance organization (HMO):** This is a network of health providers from which a patient typically selects a primary care provider and then that doctor makes referrals to specialists within the network as needed.
  - **Preferred provider organization (PPO):** Similar to an HMO—a network of care providers but often does not require selecting a primary care physician for referrals to specialists.
  - **Medicare:** A federally sponsored insurance plan for people over 65 or those with certain qualifying disabilities.

- **Medicaid:** A joint federal-state plan that covers low-income patients.

  In addition to health insurance plans, there are pharmacy benefit managers that negotiate drug prices on behalf of patients and insurance plans. During the verification phase of the RCM process, the provider quickly determines what sort of coverage a patient has that will determine how they ultimately bill. A not too uncommon issue arises when a patient selects a provider that is out of network—not part of the care network covered by their insurance. This is important to flag very early; otherwise, the claim filed will be rejected and the provider will need to engage in what will likely be a drawn-out process to be compensated for services provided.

- **Coding:** All aspects of care that is provided must be properly coded to ensure that there is sufficient documentation to support the claim. This is a time-consuming process and one that providers dread. But it's also a point of failure if not done properly and shortly after the point of care/consultation. There are software packages, scanning tools, and devices that help with this step. But in the end, it still comes back to timely and accurate entry.

- **Claims submission:** The submission process is largely dictated by the payer, such as Medicare, private insurance companies, and so on. The traditional model is payment based on volume of services provided. This is rapidly changing to a value-based model where payment is based on the quality of the outcome.

- **Payment processing:** Because RCM is quite complex, it's not uncommon to have denials in claims. The claim might be declined outright due to out-of-network services or there might be partial denials based on improper coding or disagreements on the prescribed cost of the item/service being claimed. During this phase, the patient's deductible is factored in as well as any possible co-pay. *(Note: for discrete and well-defined services such as physician diagnosis, the co-pay can be identified at the point of intake/eligibility. Patients are then asked to make the co-pay payment before the procedure/appointment takes place. This has a positive impact on cash flow for the provider.)*

- **Collections:** Once the payers (insurance companies/government) determine their share of coverage they will remit to the providers. State law often specifies when the claim must be paid, imposing penalty fees for late payments. If the patient owes a portion, bills will be sent to them and a collection process will ensue. This can be drawn out if the amount is large and the patient is unable to pay. This is where many providers run into problems with cash recovery.

Makayla knew from a very young age that she wanted to be a doctor. Her mother was her hero. An immigrant who came to America from Tanzania, her mother overcame barrier after barrier and dedicated her life to providing care for people in a rural town in Missouri. With her other highly accomplished friends, Makayla downplays her success as a surgeon, describing herself as a simple country doctor. In reality the person she admires the most in the world was in fact a simple country doctor.

"Ladies, I've had enough of you. Time to leave!" Makayla said with dramatic flair.

"Well, I'm glad you said what we've all been thinking," Paulette returned the playful banter.

Summary

As Carol drove home that night, she had a smile on her face. "Not bad for a girl from Sweetwater, Tennessee," she said aloud to herself, thinking about her dear friends and how far she had come in her career. It had been a rewarding few weeks for Carol. When she first approached Bob about Owens's cash position, she wasn't entirely sure how he would react. She knew he would understand and respect her suggestions, but he got very engaged on a personal level. She and Bob had been through the trenches as they helped grow the company and she always knew him to be a man who would roll up his sleeves and get involved.

But lately he had been focusing so much on growing Owens. She thought it might be reasonable to expect him to delegate things to her. But he didn't do that. He jumped right in, meeting with key stakeholders, reviewing data, and sending a signal to the rest of the leadership team that cash is equally important. Owens can't achieve its aspirations without significant capital investment. Bob quickly understood that and provided the type of leadership that only a CEO can do. Now all of the management team not only understands the importance of cash but also they are starting to see how their decisions affect results and who has decision rights, focusing on helping the extended organization make necessary trade-offs.

Time will tell if the cash leadership office (CLO) will really make the impact that they hope it will. But she knows her boss well and recognizes that if Bob is committed to something, it gets done. He told the board and the company at large that Owens will focus on revenue growth, cost containment, and cash generation. Three legs of the stool. "Cash is king," Bob said at the all-hands meeting. He even had a customized doormat made with that slogan. He placed it in the hall outside the door to the conference room that is the command center for the CLO.

"This is how a CFO makes a difference," Carol said out loud as she drove home.

Acknowledgments

I am so fortunate to have spent my career with brilliant people who challenge me, helping me grow and learn. I wish I could name them all, but special thanks to Steve Payne, Mark Tennant, Hye Yu, Henri Van der Eerden, Peter Rabjohns, Stuart Douglas, Nick Boaro, Patrick Lee, Sven Braun, Marcus Homeyer, Arthur James, Albert Leguizamo, Shawn Ryan, Eidji Braghin, Gerardo Gonzalez, Melissa Orsi, Carson Bricco, Uma Chidambaram, Deepak Jayanti, Logan Dungan, and Dan Gravelle.

And to my family, I am ever grateful for your love and support: Thom Lambert, Gordon and Kathleen Kingma, Dave and Annette Moore, Stan and Marilyn Kingma, Randy and Cheryl Bice, Steve and Kathy Glover, Nancy Rodrique, Chuck and Nancy Wall.

About the Author

Peter W. Kingma leads the working capital practice in the Americas for Ernst & Young LLP. With 30+ years of experience, he advises global companies on all aspects of cash management across several sectors, including manufacturing, consumer products, retail, aerospace, and defense. He has written on the topic for several business publications. Peter earned a BS in economics from Purdue University and lives in Chicago, Illinois, and Columbia, Missouri.

Index